In praise of
111 INSPIRATIONAL LIFE PURPOSE QUOTES . . .

"In *111 Inspirational Life Purpose Quotes & Exercises to Find Your Purpose in Life,* you have been given an effective tool for your life's journey created from over 30 years of Suzanne's quest for truth while examining every teacher, practice, and theory possible. Her own struggles have informed her teaching and created not a road map but a GPS for those who want to take the path to purpose in their life. Now YOU just have to turn it on!"

~ Terry J. Basile
Private Practice, Marriage & Family Therapist

"What a beautifully practical tool Suzanne has created. *111 Inspirational Life Purpose Quotes & Exercises to Find Your Purpose in Life* is chock-full of practical applications for how we can find the guru within. The exercises can build upon themselves in a linear fashion or stand alone as individual lessons that call out to the longing within your soul . . . Dare to discover who you really are!"

~ Karen Malone, M.S.

"Suzanne takes you on a fabulous journey in which she guides you with 111 tools to help you choose the path from which you will gain your own personal wisdom. Unlock YOUR true purpose in life! Thank you for your tremendous insight, dear Goddess . . . for you I am eternally thankful."

~ Mary Prantil, Artist, Sierra Visions

"Whether you are considering your life purpose for the first time or wanting to expand upon your current purpose, this book is full of treasures. The author demonstrates her understanding of the human journey by bringing forth a broad spectrum of tools for self-discovery."

~ Kari Carter

"Whether you are a young adult just starting out in life or you are approaching midlife, this book will take you by the hand and gently help you understand your higher calling. It is a book of divine intervention itself. Whether you are a successful business executive or a homemaker, this book is a good exercise in understanding your true self and your unique life's purpose."

~ Nicola Davis

"For years, I struggled to find my purpose. Many trials and tribulations would overtake me while on my journey. However, in a person's life, there are things that give you pause and make you take note. It happens when someone or something crosses our path, and it just seems we are ready to WAKE UP. I recently had the opportunity to find *111 Inspirational Life Purpose Quotes and Exercises to Find Your Purpose in Life.* Had I had this workbook earlier, my life would have been so much simpler. Do yourself a favor, obtain your own copy of this PEACE of work, and stop just passing through this life—begin to live it and live it on purpose."

~ Karen Mayfield, Founder of Wake Up Women

"This book is meant to provide a clear focus, meaning and direction to your life, and it does so without a hitch."

~ Dr. Olivia Dsouza

"*111 Inspirational Life Purpose Quotes and Exercises to Find Your Purpose in Life* is a step-by-step workbook created by a highly trained specialist who uses exercises augmented with uplifting phrases for a positive mindset that starts the process of positive transformation. What I find exceptional about Suzanne Strisower's unique transformational method is how it teaches readers to embrace a new way of processing thoughts and emotions for a complete mindshift. This process is made available in an interactive workbook that is inviting in color, format, and symbolism. During this course, readers embark on a journey of self-discovery that allows them to progress at their own pace. I found that discovering and fulfilling my life purpose lead to a happier, healthier, and more fulfilling life."

~ Kathleen O'Keefe Kanavos, author

"*111 Inspirational Life Purpose Quotes and Exercises to Find Your Purpose in Life* by Suzanne Strisower is not just another book on the rather cluttered self-help bookshelf. It makes you think. Actually formulating our life purpose is something that few of us do. We tend to drift along and seek valuation from our salaries or our shoe collections. Strisower makes us sit up and take stock of where we are in life and forces us to see how much more fulfilling we could be making our lives. That is not as daunting as it sounds; with her guidance, we can all become lifestyle entrepreneurs who are passionate and purposeful in what we do.

"Strisower casts a wide net and brings in elements of mystic energy and spirituality into the mix, together with career, practical, and psychological assessments. Even the greatest self-help skeptic will find some interesting food for thought in this intriguing and well-constructed book."

~ Stephanie Dagg

"Wow, Suzanne! What an amazing book. Brilliantly written and enjoyable to read. I love the interactiveness that you provided throughout the book through lessons that are structured in such a way that you get complete clarity and understanding of what your life purpose is.

"I found the step-by-step process simple to follow, and I couldn't put the book down until I finished it. It was very exciting to read. I had been feeling a bit disconnected to my life purpose over the past while and wasn't sure why.

"Just two days after reading your book, I was doing my morning meditation when the words 'your purpose' came to me. I wasn't really sure what it meant at first, so I just listened. In that moment I was given a new life purpose.

"It felt very personal as the words came through, and I realized that I felt totally connected and aligned to this purpose. I knew in my heart that this was truly my reason for being here.

"Thank you, Suzanne, for inspiring me and for the contribution you made to my life and everyone else who will be affected by this book."

—Vera Stark, Westwold, BC, Canada
Coach and Healer, www.EmotionalLifeCoaching.com

111 Inspirational Life Purpose Quotes & Exercises to Find Your Purpose in Life

---

A Workbook to Be Your Best Self & Live Your Best Life

Suzanne Strisower, M.A., PCC

Spirit, Nature & YOU ❖ Oroville, CA

Printed in the United States of America in February 2013.

This workbook is designed and published by:

Suzanne Strisower, M.A., PCC

Spirit, Nature & YOU

Box 559, Oroville, CA 95965

Suzanne@YourNextStepCoach.com

www.YourNextStepCoach.com

530-589-5889

Acknowledgments

There are many people and beings I want to acknowledge—those living and those on the other side. Two of the most important people who helped make vision and their expression possible were my parents—Edward and Beverly Strisower—who transitioned long before they could see the vision that I have struggled for decades to articulate finally manifest. Thanks for always telling me that it was possible and for having faith in me, even when you had no idea what I was talking about.

To the two most important Beings to me on the other side, Great Spirit-Archangel Uriel—my lifelong guide and mentor, I don't know what I would have done without you. You guided me brilliantly with love and patience, even when I was clueless and defiant, always allowing me free will while not letting me hurt myself. To my beloved Arjuna, my true love and loyal spiritual warrior, you made the journey worthwhile and kept me on track in a way I have not allowed any human to do. Thank you—I love and miss you.

To those in this dimension who have been so supportive of me. John David Hensley, who has grounded and seen me through my dark nights of the soul—you made it all possible. To my Star Sisters—Linda Fleischman, Lynn Bachus, Jude Johnston, Andrea Dawn Wilson, and Laura Denney—who truly got my work. To my dear sister, Ana Klatt-Mogro, for her brilliant light, to Aletha Kauthue—my eternal spiritual mother, and to Terry Basile, who has always encouraged my efforts.

To my dear editor, Lori Glenn, who made the editing process feel good, and the manuscript benefited from her diligent and conscious editing. To my Lightwork friend and coach, Vera Stark, thanks for reframing the hard parts of the lifestyle entrepreneur's journey into a positive for me. Kira Freed did an extraordinary job of making this manuscript beautiful and elegant, giving it the polish and beauty to make it sing to your heart. To Joshua and Summer Price for your generosity in channeling my beautiful life purpose logo for the cover, and to Lani Phillips of Wise Women Ink, who gave me the front cover concept without ever having been asked.

To my many clients, who make expansion visible and who have given me faith that what I have to offer indeed makes sense and makes a difference in your lives. Special thanks to Mary, Sharon, and my Platinum Pod group, Revs. Bill and Geri, and my Fairy Godparents, Dean and Louise, for your support and love, and to many others who have crossed my path. My profound appreciation for your impact on my life!

Dedication

111 Inspirational Life Purpose Quotes & Exercises to Find Your Purpose in Life is dedicated to my parents in Spirit, to Arjuna, and to Great Spirit ~ Archangel Uriel. I am ready to step out and "Be the Golden Ray" of light I incarnated to be in this world, which you have all so patiently and lovingly nurtured along . . .

The cover logo, which is also on the top of each page, symbolizes how your life purpose weaves through every aspect and expression of your life. It also reflects the mind-body-spirit and emotional connection we have when we live from our purpose.

This workbook is dedicated to all the 3D individuals (people functioning day-to-day) who know there is more to themselves and life, but just not where to go to expand. This workbook will help you express your life purpose and manifest your true potential!

This workbook is dedicated to people who want to connect with their 4D (people who can listen to their intuition, Higher Self, and guidance) spiritual beings. This is a wonderful midpoint in the journey when your intuition starts to guide you, and it's where things start to get interesting.

This workbook is dedicated to those individuals who KNOW they are 5D lightworkers and who want to live in the vibration of that conscious awareness. It offers a glimpse into the possibility of your 5D vibration (the next evolutionary step we are all taking to become beings of light) as Light Beings!

Enjoy the journey and let this workbook guide you forward in your experience of the "D's"—dimensions through which we are all traveling at warp speed on the planet now. I hope it will bring together and embody for you all the different expressions of your Life Purpose . . .

Table of Contents

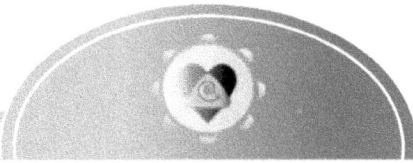

Introduction

111 Inspirational Quotes & Exercises to Find Your Purpose in Life evolved over several years. I have watched people's hunger to find their life purpose grow from a novelty concept into something that guides their lives—natally, developmentally, psychologically, professionally, spiritually, mystically, and transitionally. This workbook will help people truly understand and articulate their life purpose from each of these perspectives. The seven sections of exercises are divided in half, with sixty exercises exploring the developmental, practical, psychological, and professional, and fifty-one exercises tapping into the intuitive and energetic.

People who know their life purpose are more directed and fulfilled in their lives because they have a path on which they can consciously journey. Simply, a life purpose is what we consciously put our life force energy into knowing, accomplishing, and fulfilling.

Definition of Life Purpose

Merriam-Webster's Collegiate Dictionary defines *purpose* as an "aim, intention, or to put forth." Therefore, one understanding of your life purpose is what you're putting your energy into or the aim or intention of all your external efforts.

For example, let's say you have a practical intention to be a good mother. Your life purpose might manifest as helping your children become self-sufficient, independent, conscious human beings by nurturing their interests, not what you or society thinks they should do or be. Or you could be an artist who dedicates your life to making beautiful creations out of trash, and your life purpose is to help people become conscious of their waste and creative ways to reuse it rather than just unconsciously discarding unwanted items.

Spiritually, your life purpose could be to fulfill a karmic debt or to do something that the Divine has guided or commanded you to do, such as Moses leading his people. Each person's purpose is valuable and contributes something to life and to the well-being of the planet. No matter how small or large, it helps to fulfill that mission.

Deepak Chopra, in his book *The Seven Spiritual Laws of Success,* offers three practical criteria to know that you have found your life purpose:

- It's a unique gift or talent that you have in this life.

- You know how to use that talent in some type of service.

- It must, in some way, benefit humanity and the planet.

Each individual's true life purpose will fulfill these three criteria. You can use the examples in the previous paragraph to intellectually understand how each action is the fulfillment of a life purpose when it meets these three criteria. People each have a purpose to fulfill, even if they aren't aware of the long-term impact or the outcome of their actions. They are motivated by the desire to fulfill their life purpose using their true potential in the world.

Your Developmental Stage & Its Impact on Your Life Purpose

The developmental and physical stages of our lives are hardwired into each of us. These experiences are purposeful and can best be articulated through Maslow's Hierarchy of Needs. Abraham Maslow, an American psychologist, described how, in each of eight phases of life, a person is fulfilling one of the eight basic needs. These basic needs could be construed as the purpose that needs to be expressed in that stage. The stages start with fulfilling our survival needs and evolve through our lives until we reach the final stage of transcendence.

This natural starting point for finding one's life purpose is something that each of us struggles with and strives for. We can also fluctuate between stages if we have a catastrophic event—such as a death, a home fire, loss of income, loss of a spouse, or a near-death experience—that causes us to reevaluate our purpose for being and what to do next. The expression of your life purpose changes over the course of your lifetime; you naturally do not want the same things at twenty that you do at sixty or seventy. Each life stage has evolutionary milestones that want to be expressed, mastered, and integrated into your life.

I devised a chart called "The Developmental Stage of Life Purpose" (see Section 1, Exercise #1, page 30), which is modeled on Maslow's Hierarchy of Needs and takes into account each area of your life: Profession/Career, Personal Growth/Spiritual Development, Fun/Rest and Relaxation, Physical Health/Overall Well-Being, Environments/Home and Work, and Relationships/Primary and Peer. Each aspect has a way to evolve and grow in that particular stage. This learning, which is woven in with your purpose, takes you from the basics of establishing your life through individuation, the process of developing skills to thrive on your own, to the other end of the life span of leaving a legacy and experiencing transcendence.

Your professional and career endeavors generate transitions that you go through during your life span. Your purpose involves using your natural skills, gifts, talents, and passions in some concrete way. An example of your professional evolution is starting as an apprentice carpenter and then becoming a journeyman carpenter, which leads you into an area of specialization such as high-end finish work. As you age, generally in your 40s and beyond, you then look at other ways to express the best of who you are that are personally fulfilling, often with a desire to be of service to something bigger than yourself. During your midlife transition, reevaluation, or "midlife crisis," you are not sure where to go from here. You have long ago completed the current stage, which now restricts you personally, professionally, and spiritually. The carpenter during this process realizes that he can no longer work for someone else and decides to start his own business, specializing in the particular type of finish work that he is known for and has a passion for.

Transitions ~ Midlife & Beyond

The later parts of this conscious journey are for those who have reached middle age or beyond who are now focused on mortality and leaving a legacy, which becomes another mission or purpose to fulfill. This search can arise as a result of numerous reasons—family legacies, tragedies, a mission you want to accomplish, or something in your heart that yearns to be fulfilled. Each of these reasons is an expression of your life purpose, whether or not you are conscious of it.

At the other end of the continuum is your spiritual Self and divine purpose. This aspect of you may wait until you are ready to explore it, or if you have a spiritual side that you have been developing over the course of your life, it will be present concurrently with each developmental stage and will be expressed through every aspect of your life, career, and daily activities.

Your purpose will run through each of the eight stages of your life, but it can have many different expressions throughout your life, depending on the phase you are in. The first section of this workbook is tangible, chronological, and psychological because these are the most easily recognized and understood parts of yourself. Everything from your basic interests as a child to your current hobbies as an adult are resources that can be used to understand your life purpose.

Your life purpose won't change during your lifetime, but the way you express it might. As an example, as a teenager, I started doing professional psychic readings. Later, I wanted to support people in ways that helped them know and empower themselves through my work as a life coach. All along, my purpose has been to empower people and help them connect to their own guidance and spiritual side. Proverbially, I want to teach people how to fish rather than simply giving them some spiritual fish or insights.

Your Life Purpose Is Multifaceted

People often feel frustrated because they don't know "where to find their purpose" or "how to know they've 'found' their life purpose." Your purpose in life is bigger than you are and is multifaceted in nature.

Your life purpose is both practical—requiring you to do something and requiring the best of who you are—and spiritual, as every part of your being participates in accomplishing it. There is a divine and inspired quality to your life purpose, no matter what it is. Think of all the people you know who are "on a mission." There is an exalted awareness and an honoring that you feel about fulfilling whatever your purpose asks of you. It is always something positive that supports and sustains life.

Emotionally, people who have found their life purpose feel a sense of relief, knowing they have a focus and direction from within that guides their life. This clarity and direction helps them know what decision to make and what path to follow.

Your life purpose is bigger than an action—it is an orientation that I believe can be expressed or understood from the perspectives of three different dimensions:

- 3D includes our tangible physical reality, the events or things we create with our life force energy, and what our actions and goals are trying to accomplish.

- 4D is an awareness and connection to the unseen, intuitive, divine, and karmic aspects of our purpose. This dimension is where most of us try to find our life purpose through the many personal growth and spiritual development approaches available from major new thought leaders, such as Pastor Rick Warren, to Native Americans to Buddhists.

- 5D is much more expansive and is not easily articulated. It is the energy of the "New Age" or "Great Shift" that is coming in, and it is a conscious light frequency—a vibration we can embody that impacts everything it comes in contact with. 5D encompasses the 3D and 4D purposes as well as being fused with the energy of one's Being as an energy field, like that of a guru. People experience the 5D in peak or mystical experiences.

The spiritual component of your life purpose is a vision or guidance that you are following, a feeling of "being led" and a sense of knowing from deep within what you are here to do. In my own life, I was told to write a screenplay about my life because, as Great Spirit told me, "Humanity is suffering, and it needs to see what a life of spirit and possibility look like."

We as a species experience all these levels of purpose—from 3D "doing" to 4D "knowing" to 5D "being" or transcendence as human beings. The first peoples had this connection with the cosmos and their physical places. Now, as a species, we are starting to expand our consciousness in a new way—as multidimensional beings. The next three pages describe what an "exalted" life purpose might be through each of the dimensions. Your exalted purpose in life represents the ideal expression possible for you in each area of your life.

3D ~ Becoming a Lifestyle Entrepreneur

Many professionals and other people are entering a period of reevaluating their lives and their priorities. This phase—whether it is age/stage related, a midlife crisis, being a professional in transition, having a change in job status, or having reached a plateau—is a time to reassess your values, direction in life, career, and profession. People want to have their life purpose expressed in what they do. Are you fulfilled and satisfied by your current endeavors?

Oftentimes the answer to this question is NO. As a result, people begin a personal quest to find whatever will create meaning and fulfillment in their lives. Being clear about one's life purpose can help guide a person in determining what is important and fulfilling to him or her. One of the new ways to address this is by opting out of conventional work and becoming a "lifestyle entrepreneur."

What Are Lifestyle Entrepreneurs?

Lifestyle entrepreneurs are people who have carved out a unique path for themselves—their own schedules and their own orientation to the field. They no longer care about being a financial success or a "superstar" or being "driven by success." They want to use their skills and energy in ways that provide personal meaning, purpose, and fulfillment on their own terms. These people are passionate and purposeful about what they do and how they do it; they opted out of the corporate world because it didn't embody their passion and sense of purpose.

Steps to Transitioning into Being a Lifestyle Entrepreneur

1. Identify your life purpose. What are you here to do?
2. Understand how best to express your life purpose using your unique skills, passions, and expertise.
3. Research possible options and venues for yourself—consulting, coaching, a new business venture, and so on.
4. Consider various funding options—savings, retirement accounts, unemployment benefits, loans, and so on.
5. Create an action plan to launch yourself as a lifestyle entrepreneur in your chosen profession, market, and venue.

I recommend using this action plan to bring all your energy and focus to make it happen in order to create a happy and satisfying life doing what you love most and fulfilling your life purpose. As a lifestyle entrepreneur, you have the opportunity to do things that energize and express your passion and purpose for a living.

4D ~ New Awareness & Purpose for Being

Owen Waters, in his book *The Shift: The Revolution in Human Consciousness,* concludes, "It is a part of the plan of the Infinite Being that we progress to the next stage of conscious human evolution." "The Shift" is the most wonderful transformation in recorded history. This is where humanity gets to build—literally—"Heaven on Earth." Our magnificent blueprint and expanded awareness help us participate in the bigger picture through the journey of our personal lives as it expresses and manifests our purpose. Below are Waters' "Twelve Principles for the New Reality." Each aspect relates to your purpose and the reconnection with your Higher Self or Infinite Being in this lifetime.

1. *Infinite Being is All That Is.* Everything exists within this consciousness.

2. *We are Infinite Beings.* Everything is part of the living hologram; each of us is a part of the whole.

3. *Purpose in life.* These are the personal themes you choose to experience in this lifetime and as the Infinite Being experiencing itself through you.

4. *Free will enables you to explore your true potential.* You are free to choose how to uniquely express your purpose and potential and live your life.

5. *Reincarnation.* A variety of experiences are created through each unique incarnation.

6. *Life after 'death.'* Reflecting on your last life from the spirit realm's perspective gives you a broader experience of who you truly are.

7. *Life reflects what you project.* Karma is an aspect of the mirror of what you project into the world that comes back to you.

8. *Abundance is natural.* You are in the flow, being your best self and following your inner joy.

9. *Love is the only reality.* Unconditional love and acceptance toward ourselves and all things are the underlying purposes for being.

10. *Self-responsibility* involves being responsible for the experience and reality you create for yourself.

11. *Truth is everywhere.* Direct experience offers the ultimate truth moment by moment.

12. *Inner connection and insight* involve connecting with your spiritual source.

5D ~ Lightwork: The Purpose for Being

The first question a person might ask is "What is a lightworker or light being?"

Lightworkers are people whose purpose is in service to a "higher power" or to higher dimensional energies. They are vibrating and living from the core of their being. Their life purpose is to bring these higher frequencies of consciousness and light to the planet. It is done by helping people on the planet awaken and wake up their "lightbody." It is not a clearly articulated purpose, as is the case with 3D and 4D purposes. A 5D life purpose involves helping the planet evolve in whatever ways a person is called into service moment by moment. Some common 5D lightworker examples are:

1. People who work with the ascended masters and vibrate specific frequencies on the planet as their purpose. They could be following a guru, be connected with an ascended master, or be working with the archangels.
2. People working to shift the duality of the planet back into harmony.
3. People who help awaken and elevate the consciousness of others.
4. People who spontaneously presence the divine spark of life and light in themselves and others.
5. People who live in the Dreamtime and who have a deep connection with Nature.
6. People who dedicate their lives to "service"—to something bigger than themselves.
7. People who are focused on being and who are not attached to doing or accomplishing anything besides being in service to the divine frequencies.

Many lightworkers may have felt awkward in this lifetime due to being totally misunderstood because they are not goal oriented or materialistic by nature. They want things on the planet to be in right order and to help people who are suffering. Lightworkers have been around for eternity as saints, gurus, Christ figures, and others who are trying to help humanity reach a more loving, compassionate place of being. They have long ago renounced attachments to the material world and pleasures of the flesh. Some great examples are Mother Teresa, Buddha, shamans, and medicine men/women.

It's time for each person to be empowered and have clarity about his or her purpose for a fulfilling life by doing something meaningful that makes a difference to the quality of life on our amazing Mother Earth.

What is your life purpose? Can you see how your life purpose has a multidimensional quality to it? If not, it's time to explore and open up to the dimensional nature of your Being and its magnificent life purpose!

Finding Your Life Purpose

How long have you spent trying to figure out your life purpose? What is your life purpose from the 3D, 4D, and 5D perspectives? How will you know when you have found your life purpose? Do these questions sound familiar? Is this something you want to know NOW?

With the coming New Age, it is important that each of us know our exalted purpose—to know why each of us chose to incarnate at this particular time. Your purpose will guide you through these turbulent times by helping you ascertain what you are supposed to be focusing on. You are a seed of the Divine who has come here to help humanity and the planet. Each person has a purpose that is important and needed at this time.

I recommend doing the exercise sections in this workbook consecutively, starting with the developmental, then the assessments, onto the practical and psychological, and so forth. The reason for this is that you will consciously follow 3D "the known in your world" information, which progressively deepens into the 4D guidance of your purpose, to finally being your 5D lightbeing as your purpose.

Use this book both practically and intuitively. I recommend that you do exercises from each section to gain the broadest perspective for truly knowing your purpose and how you are meant to express it. I have included exercises for several different learning styles to tailor your experience to how you most effectively receive information. You can also choose exercises by what you feel most inspired to do and see what arises out of the ones you choose.

From the Practical to Your Divine Beingness

This workbook is designed with several different perspectives in mind. It has a continuum of possibilities in order for you to explore various ways to find your purpose. I have provided 111 different ways to inspire, examine, and discover your life purpose. They are broken into sections so you can work by areas of interest or by the stage of life you are currently in. This workbook is uniquely ordered from personal to the spiritual/cosmic as well as from several vantage points. I recommend that you do them sequentially to deepen and expand your experience and get the most from the natural order and flow. Another approach is to follow your own interests or guidance and do the exercises that feel most relevant to you.

I encourage you to do at least 25 of the exercises so you can experience your life purpose from many different angles or randomly pick a page each day. The goal of this workbook is to give you clarity about your purpose to guide your life from many different viewpoints. The sections in this workbook are presented in the following order:

1. The developmental stages of the Hierarchy of Needs

2. Your "birth" purpose through your name, numerology, and astrology through free websites. (People love this section and find it very validating.)

3. The psychological and practical—your likes, dislikes, and psychological assessments

4. Your professional and career expressions of your unique gifts, talents, and your sense of your purpose in doing them

5. Spiritual and contemporary new thought leaders from many perspectives, including New Age, spiritual, and human potential movement teachers such as Eckhart Tolle, Deepak Chopra, and many others. Sacred texts from various spiritual and religious traditions as well as some information on reincarnation are also included.

6. The cosmological and "lightworker," as expressed in nature and by the aboriginal or first people's perspective and the eternal as presenced in One's beingness

7. Transitions and midlife reassessments for people who are at a crossroads—personal, professional, retirement, legacy—and how they give purpose to it

Remember the old adage "There are no accidents." When you get to the other side of knowing your Life Purpose and Inner Gifts, you will see how perfectly laid out everything in your life has been for what you are here to do.

Knowing You've Found Your Life Purpose

You will know when you have connected to your Life Purpose because all of a sudden, a light will turn on inside you. It will be an epiphany or a series of small resonances, all pointing in the same direction, that finally say—*I know my purpose!* There can also be a sense of elation and, in the next breath, a powerful sense of being overwhelmed by the magnificence and scale of that vision and purpose. Relax—you can accomplish your life purpose in stages. Remember, you have been preparing for an eternity for this moment to manifest your Gifts. The results you will experience include:

• Your purpose will give clarity, focus, and direction to your life.

• You will understand the meaning and purpose behind how you spend your time and energy.

• Sensitive people who know you well will say that this seems like a natural next step for you to be taking.

• Validation from others might sound like, "I've known that about you all along" or "You seem really happy and suited to what you are doing."

• Your Spirit and Soul will finally feel seen, and there will be a warmth in your heart.

Internally, you might have a feeling of "rightness." A vast amount of emotional energy appears when you finally have clarity and feel seen. Everything will seem to flow; there's a sense of momentum, and you can become quite energized by what you are doing. Everything you've done before now helps you succeed in expressing your Life Purpose using your Inner Gifts. The benefits you'll receive from going through this book and its exercises are the synthesis of your insight and understanding; knowing your Life Purpose and Inner Gifts, which creates a sense of Freedom; and a feeling of Power and Conviction about who you are and what you are here to do.

Buddha left a roadmap,

Jesus left a road map,

Krishna left a road map,

Rand McNally left a road map.

But you still have to travel the road yourself.

~ Stephen Levine, *Who Dies?*

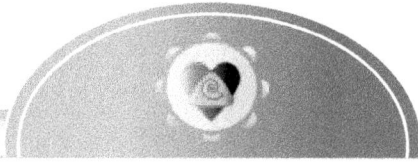

111 Inspiring Quotes & Exercises of Purpose

The best way to bring your Life Purpose and Inner Gifts to light is to do each exercise in order to explore your Self from many different perspectives. Read each quote and contemplate its intent, then use the exercise to deepen and personalize the quote as it applies to your purpose. Each exercise will either bring insight and direction or concepts that have no relevance to you; either way, it is valuable to rule things in or out. It is also a great way for you to understand how you fit into the bigger world.

Let's Get Started ~ Here Are Your Instructions

1. Work through the first section of the workbook, on your Developmental Stage, which will help you immediately understand your human developmental and chronological goals and purpose.

2. Synthesize your answers and insights from this section and write them down on page 165. Use this page as a synthesis page to journal and reveal whatever you have discovered from the exercises you have completed in that section about your life purpose. Do the visualizations to bring further clarity to the manifestation of your Gifts.

3. Move into the section(s) that are relevant to you—the Natal to discover your cosmic blueprint; the Psychological, with the Free Online Tools and Assessments to understand your personality and preferences; the Professional to know your specific skills, gifts and talents; the Transitional or Midlife to understand where you are and what is important to you at this time in your life; the Spiritual to understand your divine or inner calling; or the Mystical to know who you are energetically. Do at least five exercises in each section so you will have done a minimum of twenty-five exercises. Do however many exercises it takes until you start to see the redundancy in your answers, for example, "Yes, I like to do _____, and it keeps showing up again and again in my answers."

4. Look at the repetitive insights and epiphanies that the exercises yield in order to articulate your purpose to yourself. Ask yourself WHY, which reflects the reasons or your underlying purpose in life.

A wonderful example of this process took place when a coach read this book cover to cover and then went to bed for the night. She didn't do a single exercise but awoke totally clear about her purpose.

If you engage the process, you will be rewarded with clarity and excitement, and you'll know your true purpose in life, too!

Section 1 ~ Your Developmental Purpose ~ What Stage Are You At in Life?

The first section of this workbook describes those parts of our lives that everyone has in common: the "Hierarchy of Needs," which Maslow defined as the steps each person needs to take from "Basic Truth" and survival skills to "Self-Realization." There are eight steps through which we progress as we grow older. The first chapter outlines these steps and offers a chronological timeline called "Stages of Fulfillment" plus the first exercise, "Your Developmental Stage Life Purpose" on page 30. This process is universal because everyone experiences it regardless of gender, culture, or socioeconomic background. For some people, this will be an easy process because they are self-aware; for others, it might be more difficult to discern because they are still getting to know themselves. You can also vacillate between steps. This is an unfolding process that gets richer the further you go. Be easy on yourself . . .

Section 2 ~ Your Natal Purpose ~ The Purpose You Were Born With

This section explores those qualities that come from "something bigger than yourself." Your name, numerology chart, and astrology chart were all given to you at the moment of your birth. They create a cosmic blueprint of your energies at the moment you entered this incarnation. What purposes are revealed to you in your "natal chart(s)"? I have provided websites for both Far Eastern (Chinese) astrology and traditional Western astrological charts. What are the gifts of your name and its vibration? You will learn your predispositions, which provide glimpses into your purpose. Note: Over time, some websites may change; if so, search the topic for other free website options of the same type. (People have gained a lot of insight and validation about their life purpose from this section alone.)

Section 3 ~ Your Psychological Purpose ~
Practical & Psychological Aspects of Who You Are

This section contains personality or psychological assessments and the ancient Enneagram, a Sufi psychological test for understanding one's self. The Enneagram explores what you want—to be, do, or have. The exercises are meant to help you articulate your personal preferences and focus on the direction in which you have found yourself going. There are innumerable reasons for the direction you are going, each of which is valid and perfect for your becoming.

Section 4 ~ Your Professional Purpose ~ Your Skills, Gifts, Expertise, & Career

Your career is the culmination and use of all your professional skills, talents, and preferences as well as what you have accomplished with them. This section has you focus on each part of that equation to articulate what and why you have done what you've done professionally during your working life.

Section 5 ~ Your Transitional Purpose ~ Your Next Steps, Midlife, & Beyond

People can be in transition at any age, but transitions are of particular concern to people approaching midlife, when they have lived about half their lives but still have much to experience. Any transition can reveal your purpose—as a longing, legacy, or unfinished business that you need to address or express as your purpose in life for your next chapter, second act, or encore career.

Section 6 ~ Your Spiritual Purpose ~ Your Intuition & Divine Guidance

For some, this section could be viewed as esoteric and not their common orientation toward life. However, this section contains quotations about purpose by many of the current new thought leaders including Sonia Choquette, Michael Bernard Beckwith, Joan Borysenko, Deepak Chopra, Kimberly Fulcher, and Dan Millman, as well as some religious figures such as Pastor Rick Warren, Dr. John-Roger, Thomas Mails of the Native American path, and Swami Muktananda. This section looks at the unseen aspects of your purpose, inner calling, or divine guidance.

For people who believe in past lives and regression work, this section will be especially fun. I have included numerous guided visualizations so you can explore *why* you incarnated this lifetime—which is another expression or version of a person's life purpose—to complete something that wasn't finished in a past life. The "Higher Self" is the all-knowing part of ourselves that has come into this unique lifetime with the intent to experience certain things or to bring certain qualities, understandings, or mastery to the planet at the time of incarnation. The "Future Self" offers a retrospective view of your life and what you have accomplished as well as how you feel about the future you have created when you have lived this life. This perspective gives you the opportunity to see if there are any things you would choose to do differently or to know how to correct your course. Your Higher Self and Future Self can help you create a direction and plan that provides insight and wisdom to guide you to your purpose.

Section 7 ~ Your Mystical Purpose ~ Your Energy & Beingness

This is the most esoteric section of the workbook. It focuses on your energetic, vibratory, or "exalted" Self. The goal of this section is to have you experience your frequency and the awareness of beingness within you. I designed the exercises in such a way as to elicit that experience. For some people, losing themselves comes from being in Nature, for others in deep meditation, and others have this experience through peak experiences where you no longer have the personal "I" or ego self.

Section 8 ~ Know Your Purpose ~ Discovery of Your Life Purpose

Your completed worksheets bring all the answers into one place (pages 165–169) to give you the opportunity to synthesize what you have been shown about your purpose through multiple lenses. As you go through each series of exercises, write the gist of your purpose as revealed through each exercise on the "Life Purpose Answer Sheet" (page 165). The goal of this sheet is to help you "see" what your life purpose is through all the different elements of your life and hone it down to your "top 10" life purpose themes.

I recommend you do a minimum of twenty-five exercises—five from each section—so you are guaranteed the broadest cross section of responses about your life purpose. This workbook is designed to be contemplative and to stretch you by offering different learning styles and opportunities to help both your superior and inferior functions and purpose to express themselves. Honor the quieter part of yourself that truly reflects the loves, passions, and divine nature of your being, which is longing to express itself and which will give you personal meaning and lead you to fulfillment when you live from it.

I have made an effort to offer exercises that each person, regardless of his or her belief system, will find interesting and useful. I recommend that you challenge yourself and explore some of the unfamiliar perspectives because that will be where the richness of your life lives.

Section 9 ~ Resources ~ Templates, Websites, & Bibliography

This section includes the mind mapping and resume templates, bibliography, and online resources. They are there to guide you and provide more information should you desire to expand this process for yourself.

In doing the research for this book, I explored many websites for additional information and resources for my readers. The question may arise, "Why not include everyone's website?" Several websites were very sales-oriented rather than information-oriented, so I chose not to include them in the resource list.

I conclude this section with more in-depth insight into who I am as a "Lifestyle Entrepreneur." I want to plant a seed with you that once you know your life purpose, the direction you choose can come from infinite possibilities, but it will always be by conscious choice because it will be a function of expressing your life purpose in the present moment.

Enjoy the Journey!

Open your mind-body-spirit and embrace what lies there for you! You will know what your life purpose is. The year 2013 ushers in the New Age of Aquarius—the "Great Shift of Consciousness," the "Wave of Love" where all life will be purposeful and heart-centered.

It is my hope that through the quotes and by doing the exercises, you will have epiphanies, insights, dreams, visions, and experiences, and you will find your Life Purpose! It's time to Celebrate Your Purpose in Life before taking the next step. Go honor and treat yourself well!

Enjoy the journey—it is so rich and rewarding!

Suzanne

Suzanne Strisower, M.A., PCC
Your Next Step Coach
Oroville, California
February 15, 2013

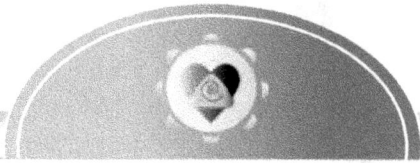

SECTION 1
Your Developmental Purpose

What Stage Are You At in Life?

- *Survival*
- *Security*
- *Social*
- *Esteem*
- *Cognitive*
- *Aesthetic*
- *Self-Actualization*
- *Transcendence*

What Stage Are You At in Life?

Every person goes through the process of self-development, although sometimes we just "go with the flow." It is my hope to make conscious the process of the human unfolding—from "individuation" through "transcendence." Individuation, as defined by Jung, means "becoming a single, homogenous being, and in so far as 'individuality' embraces our innermost, last, and incomparable uniqueness, it also implies becoming one's own self."

The other end of the continuum is self-transcendence, which A. H. Almaas, in *The Inner Journey Home,* describes as "She leaves her identity with the individual soul and becomes the boundless presence." This journey is done through a process of conscious awakening, from waking one's uniqueness to one's desire to return consciously to the Source. Maslow's Hierarchy of Needs provides a useful framework for growth and expansion to create a life of purpose and fulfillment of this evolutionary journey that each soul makes. This framework integrates the emotions and mind-body-spirit connection as well as supporting each step or decade in our developmental process. We can use these innate resources to propel us forward in our life's unfoldment.

Purpose Expressed Through the Mind-Body-Spirit Connection

Briefly defined, emotions are those feelings or actions of the heart that reflect our yearnings and passions. They can be used to sense whether we are going in the "right" direction for ourselves. The mind is our conscious compass whose job is to organize our 3D physical reality so we can best function in it. The brain's left hemisphere function puts things in order to create a plan or to execute one's life purpose. The body, another sensing organ, provides feedback to a person by its degree of relaxed openness and willingness or its rigidity and tension.

Concrete actions, both "being," like meditation, and "doing" or activity, allow people to have a different kind of feedback or insight. The Spirit's connection with each of these fundamental elements comes in multiple ways—a sense of connection with the Divine, a connection with one's own Higher Self and Future Self, a sense of connection with a network of spiritual beings, or even just a deep sense of Oneness with all things. For best results, explore as many of these connections as possible to add richness and meaning to your life. Each connection is a developmental step, from the most tangible physical needs to the most spiritual and transcendental experiences.

The stages and transitions of this journey are clearly reflected in our public and external lives. For example, in a CNN article titled "Jobs Goals by Age" (August 1, 2007), Meg Donohue discusses how

"each decade of life brings a new set of challenges as working professionals move into different phases of both their personal and professional lives." These decades can be aligned with Maslow's hierarchy to create a blueprint for people for the natural progression leading to fulfillment and success. Each person will have his or her own pace through this process.

The function of clarity and integration in one's life may be at an accelerated pace through these stages, or one may find oneself staying longer in a given phase. One's purpose can dramatically shift due to life experiences such as loss, illness, catastrophic events, changes in financial or professional circumstances, death of a spouse, child, or parent, and so on.

NOTE: The important thing to remember is that life is a journey of the soul's experience toward personal fulfillment and wholeness as articulated through this developmental needs model.

The First Way to Know Your Life Purpose ~ Your Developmental Stage

Your first way to determine your Life Purpose is by reflecting on which stage you are chronologically and functionally experiencing right now. If you have confusion about your current developmental stage and purpose due to the diverse nature of life and abilities, I have provided a chart called "Developmental Needs for Fulfillment," which shows each area of your life,. You can see where the majority of your energy is focused in Exercise #1, page 30, at the end of this section.

This interpretation of Maslow's Hierarchy of Needs correlates with stages 1 through 4 describing our 3D purpose and needs; stages 5 through 7 revealing our 4D knowing and inner purpose; and lastly, stage 8 expressing our 5D being and purpose.

Maslow's Hierarchy of Needs

Survival Needs – This period is marked by people's experience of getting their basic need for trust met, either through their parent(s) or other caregivers. On a basic level, this need includes food, clothing, and shelter; more importantly are opportunities for children to experience their surroundings, explore the world, and develop their curiosities. This will lead them to discover their innate abilities, interests, and aptitudes as well as help establish a person's basic trust or mistrust of the world.

Security Needs – This phase includes the adolescent years, when a strong inner desire emerges to individuate from caretakers and prove one's competency. As young people become more autonomous in school, they become more responsible for their own training and learning through both the educational system and direct experience. They begin to develop their own sense of self, personal preferences, and a desire to create safety and stability for themselves in their environment and the world.

Social Needs – Adults, who have ideally completed some type of formal education, apprenticeship, or vocational training, are ready to launch themselves in the world. This is a time to develop friendships, intimate relationships, and families in order to create a sense of belonging and community.

In her CNN article, Donohue states that the goal of the Social Needs stage is to "establish a positive work record"—to successfully have a first "real" job, build a skill set, and have professional connections, teamwork, and recognition of peers, all of which will help propel the person into the next phase.

Esteem Needs – Donohue refers to this phase as "focus on becoming a leader" in terms of a person's career or industry. The brilliant economist and author Tom Friedman, in *The World Is Flat*, clearly defines four ways in which a person can successfully express himself or herself in the world:

- "Special" describes people like Michael Jordan, Barbra Streisand, Bill Gates, or Oprah, who just by being themselves are unique and successful in their chosen endeavors.

- "Specialized" refers to people who are very narrowly focused and experts in their chosen area of endeavor, such as an astronaut.

- "Anchored" describes people who use their skills in a secure profession that the location will always require, such as dentists, doctors, bankers, and so on.

- "Adaptable" refers to people who work to develop transferable skills and talents that can be used in many different ways and in many different industries. Examples include computer programmers, fast food workers, and salespeople.

People who are not successful in the other three ways will still thrive if they are Adaptable. This is a time to create a more focused career path, to begin to celebrate your accomplishments, and to answer the question "Where do I fit?"

The trick is to make the most of whichever type you are professionally and to build on that. These experiences lead to a person's thriving with self-esteem, confidence, competence, respect, and recognition.

Cognitive Needs – This is generally the midpoint in a person's lifespan and a natural time to reassess—hence the possibility of a "midlife crisis" if you are not living your inspired life. Using the four types of workers mentioned in the previous section, it is possible to determine the best way to articulate your professional type—Special, Specialized, Anchored, or Adaptable—and to articulate the connection to your inner self in order to optimize your ambitions in life. Donohue feels that this

is a time to "redefine your definition of success," which includes work-life balance questions as well as questions about your career and professional options. Most importantly, the question is: What will make you feel successful? Once these questions have a purposeful resolution, there is a need to learn more, to explore, and to increase your knowledge and intelligence.

This stage is often a time of reentry for parents or a major career and life change toward a more personal sense of accomplishment and fulfillment. If this is anticipated and understood, it can often help you to move through your life with ease and avoid having a midlife crisis.

Aesthetic Needs – This decade is marked by what Donohue calls a time "to envision your future." People are now focusing on when or if they can retire and what their retirement or next stage will mean for them. It is a time to reflect honestly on their financial viability and the possibilities of how to best position themselves for retirement, both personally and professionally. This phase is marked by a need to see beauty in nature and one's self and to appreciate the order and beauty of their reality. This phase marks people's sense of success and their desire to enjoy the best that the world has to offer them.

The rest of people's lives move into the deeply personal and inner-directed needs, in that people are now inquiring more deeply to see how they can grow more, express themselves, and experience themselves in new ways. This phase may include "peak experiences" or "life-altering events" that include a spiritual component. This point is especially significant in modern times because with longer life expectancies, we are forced to redefine the meaning of our lives beyond the expectations of our parents and professions. In the stage of life when one may consider Aesthetic Needs, people who are spiritually aware are challenged to contemplate their next steps of self-actualization and transcendence.

Self-Actualization – At this stage, people experience their own personal power. Inner knowing is a quality demonstrated by the people known as "Cultural Creatives" (Exercise 10, page 45). They rely on their intuition to chart their own course—to step out autonomously on their own, in their own direction, without being bound by societal dictates. In their landmark book *The Cultural Creatives: How 50 Million People Are Changing the World,* Paul Ray and Sherry Ruth Anderson define the journey of Cultural Creatives as: "Creating a new life path, Changing the dream of success by The Inner Departure."

Step One ~ "Setting Out" allows you to learn what options are possible.

Step Two ~ "The Heart Path & Confronting the Critics" takes you on an inner journey to discover your true passion and address the critics about your chosen direction.

Step Three ~ "Distorted Mirrors, Silence about What Matters, Denial, Leading to Turning Your Values into a New Way of Life" involves a reassessment of your perceptions and a realignment to focus on a heart-centered direction, clearing out the path for new opportunities.

Step Four ~ "Creating Outside the Box, Keeping Your Eye on the Big Picture with a Passion for the Interconnectedness of Life" is the logical progression from your intimate understanding of yourself and your place in the world. Now it's time to actualize your vision in some meaningful way. For instance, Lifestyle Entrepreneurs consciously choose to express their purpose in whatever ways they are "called" to do so.

This is not a linear journey nor one we are taught in any institution. Rather, it is deeply personal and unique to each individual. It is an experience of your own self-responsibility that requires your best efforts, including your awareness, honesty, freedom, trust, legacy, and accomplishment for its own sake, not for the sake of ego gratification. Donohue refers to this as the "reap what you've sown" phase.

Self-actualization can occur at any point in your life as a result of a major event that profoundly affects you; examples include surviving a terminal illness or a catastrophic event to experiencing a deeply spiritual state where things fundamentally change inside you. People who are self-actualizing have a deeply inner-directed focus, which centers them and directs how they will interact in the world. It is a time when people have a desire to do the things they have not had time for in the past or that they want to experience while they have their vitality. Often this includes travel or peak experience activities, further education, acts of creative self-expression, creating a transition into retirement, and maximizing one's financial benefits through promotion and opportunities. Individuals have a sense of maturity and are their own self-directed authorities.

Transcendence – In this final life chapter, people focus on completions, such as any personal unfinished business from the previous decades, as well as moving in some way to connect with the Divine. This is a natural phase that helps people achieve personal growth through the use of their intuition and inner knowing, integration, and fulfillment from a place beyond their ego selves. This is an extremely intimate and personal return to the sacred at a much deeper level as people acknowledge that they are not immortal yet want to connect with the Divine. Meditation, prayer, vision quests, deep personal inquiries, or unconditional and direct communion with the Divine or God are profound, life-changing experiences that take people beyond their egos may all happen at this stage. It is a time of exalted completions, resolution, and honoring of one's life—a time to say "I've lived a good life and have made peace with this existence."

The purpose of outlining these stages of growth and change is to give people the opportunity to see the potential in their lives at the various stages and contemplate how to take advantage of it. People who get stuck in a stage can use the elements of their emotion-mind-body-spirit connection to help align them so they can move forward. For other people who may live a divinely inspired life, these stages and elements flow together effortlessly. Each stage of growth is a universal human milestone to help you track your journey of accomplishment and fulfillment.

3D ~ The Physical Expression of Our Experience of Reality

The body provides feedback in the form of vitality or lethargy and a desire to move or stay still. The body takes action as a result of the emotions it is feeling and either rises to the occasion or doesn't, depending on how well we have tended to our physical self and how aligned it is to a desired outcome. On a continuum, sensations can be experienced from restriction, contraction, or disease at one end to ease, expansiveness, and well-being in the body at the other end.

The emotions at every stage act as feedback guides for us to know if we are honoring our inner feelings and selves. When we aren't, we will experience feelings of despair, isolation, depression, and sadness. In contrast, a life in alignment with our inner self will be experienced as joyful, enthusiastic, and full of energy and zest for life. The emotions can fluctuate within this continuum many times, and there are no "bad" or "wrong" feelings. They are intended as helpful signposts to keep us in touch with ourselves. They are excellent tools to help us stay aware of our true feelings about our lives.

4D ~ The Mental & Intuitive Awareness of Our Experience of Reality

The mind as an organ of consciousness will have clarity of thought and purpose to bring forth solutions that honor our desired direction and reality. For some people, the mind functions very narrowly within focused parameters. This narrowness can create rigidity within the ego that makes the bigger picture hard to see. Creative mind mapping, brainstorming, daydreaming, and letting our minds wander are all ways to open up our thought process. This is a great opportunity to meditate and let our minds rest or to go on a vision quest with no goal beyond inner knowing.

5D ~ Our Soul's Expression of Our Being

The soul and spirit are much less tangible but equally important and powerful in our experience and quality of life. This inner and outer connection with something bigger than ourselves is profound in its presence, more than any of the other factors of life. The soul aspect is what sparks our life force energy and connects us with our own power as well as that of the Creator. It can be experienced

at any point in our life and in many different ways. Our intuition and openness will enhance this connection and foster inner peace, knowingness, and bliss.

When we are clear about our life's purpose, we experience alignment between mind, body, and spirit such that there are no internal battles or external conflicts in our lives. Examples of being incongruent include "I don't want to do it, but it would look good," "I'm not really interested in that person, but I'll go out with him anyway," "I'm really feeling fatigued, but I must go out tonight," and "I don't really want that job, but I'll take it because I may never find my dream job." Many trained professionals are available to help people return to their truth and path, including psychological professionals to help resolve underlying emotional issues and blockages, life coaches and trainers to help enhance and create life plans and articulate the path toward actualization, body workers and doctors to help with physical rejuvenation, and spiritual traditions and practitioners to connect with the Divine in whatever modality a person desires.

Your Developmental Stage Life Purpose

"Your developmental stage has a defined purpose. Which stage are you in, and what developmental purpose are you fulfilling? Every person moves through the eight stages at his or her own pace on this journey toward their wholeness and evolution."

~ Suzanne Strisower

Circle the "Stage of Purpose" that most closely fits your life focus and experience now.

Getting Your 3D Basic Needs Met

SURVIVAL ~ NEEDING TO GET YOUR BASIC NEEDS MET
Well-Being	Not being in charge of one's health, out of control
Career/Finances	No focus, menial jobs, minimum wage
Personal Growth	Trying to figure out what to do to have life work for you

STABILITY ~ WANTING TO HAVE THINGS IN ORDER
Well-Being	Conscious of health, have supportive routines
Career/Finances	A long-term job and career focus, but still just a paycheck
Personal Growth	Learning more about what "success" means for you

SOCIAL ~ WANTING TO BE MORE CONNECTED
Well-Being	Health and vibrancy, looking for more ways to be healthy
Career/Finances	Networking, knowing your way around your industry
Personal Growth	Curiosity to have a more connected and expanded world

SELF-ESTEEM ~ KNOWING YOURSELF AND HAVING SELF-WORTH
Well-Being	Being spiritually, emotionally, mentally, and physically fit
Career/Finances	Top of game, expect to be paid what you are worth
Personal Growth	Exploring areas of interest and enhancing your expertise

Exploring Your 4D Preferences & Guidance

REFINEMENT ~ CREATING BALANCE AND ORDERING THINGS FOR YOURSELF
Well-Being	Knowing yourself, tweaking your life as needed
Career/Finances	Making adjustments professionally to be more aligned with your self
Personal Growth	Learning how you want things to be, looking at your ideals

SELF-ACTUALIZATION ~ EXPLORING YOURSELF FROM THE INSIDE OUT
Well-Being	Deep connection with Self, intuition, inner wisdom
Career/Finances	Entrepreneurial, creating a personal legacy
Personal Growth	Vision quests, treks, mystical experiences, and knowledge

Flowing with Your 5D Energy & Beingness

TRANSCENDENCE ~ EXPERIENCING YOUR DIVINE CONNECTION
Relationships	GOD, CREATOR, the I AM presence, I AM, ALL THAT IS
Well-Being	Bliss state, state of grace, connected with everything
Career/Finances	Philanthropic endeavors, giving back selflessly
Personal Growth	Guides, gurus, solitary journeys, peak experiences
Rest & Relaxation	Focused awareness, state of grace and Beingness

How are you expressing that purpose now? _____

Your Natal Purpose

The Purpose You Were Born With

- *Your Name's Meaning*
- *Western Numerology*
- *African Numerology*
- *Western Astrology*
- *Chinese Astrology*

The Purpose You Were Born With

In this section, you will explore the direction and influence that come from the "composite" energy of your cosmic blueprint through the influence of your name, numerology, and astrology—all of which you "inherited" at birth as expressions of your purpose.

Your Name & Numerology Charts

The numerology chart is said to have meaning in the vibration of the sound that emanates from your given name. It comes from the name that is given to you at birth, which can either be inspired or given to you by the Divine in the naming rituals of the Hawaiians, Native Americans, or African tribes. Your name expresses the gift you are bringing to your village in this incarnation. It is interesting to note that it can be a psychological representation as well. The energy of the most common names of a particular time can represent a generational purpose. Remember when names like Brittany and Ashley were common? In an effort to offer you contrasting cultures and possibilities, I have also included an exercise to discover what your African numerology means.

Your Astrology Charts

Astrology represents a snapshot, through the birth or natal chart, of the planets at the time of your birth as well as how they were interacting with each other. These create dynamic forces that guide your life, which are present and which will influence your course of action in this lifetime. Of particular importance in your chart is the tenth house, which relates to accomplishment and your profession. This house reflects what you are recognized for in the world. Another astrological perspective comes from your Chinese astrology, which gives you the Eastern perspective.

This should create a picture or starting point for understanding the motivations and purpose with which you came into this lifetime. Each person will have a unique profile that emerges from this section's exercises. Let your mind be open to all the possibilities that are presented in order to see the tapestry that is woven for you in this lifetime as your purpose.

EXERCISE #2
Your Name's Meaning Life Purpose

"Most names do have meanings, and you should at least find out what your favorite choices mean before giving them to your child." (p. 10)

~ Bruce Lansky, *10,000 Baby Names*

In African traditions, it is believed that the name of a person carries the gift that they will be bringing to their village in this incarnation.

Look for your gift by going to www.BehindtheName.com or another online name site or book of names to find out the meaning and origins of your first name. This gives you another reference point for your purpose. What does your name mean, and how can you imagine that meaning reflecting your purpose in life in what you do or could do?

_____

_____

_____

How about your last name? Where does it come from? What do people in your family do historically? How are you demonstrating those qualities in your life?

_____

_____

_____

_____

_____

_____

_____

_____

Exercise #3
Your Numerological Life Purpose

"Numerology shows you what the vibration of your name means." Check out these FREE websites for more information about your purpose as it is expressed through your name.

~ Suzanne Strisower

Note: To get an accurate numerology reading, you need to give the site your full name at birth—not a married name, stepname, and so on.

• Go to www.affinitynumerology.com and click on their "free numerology reading." The reading is clear and concise. Note what it says for your "Destiny or Ultimate Goal" and "Your Life's Path." What did each one say about who you are?

_____

_____

_____

• Go to www.facade.com/numerology for your free numerology profile. What does your name point you toward as your purpose?

_____

_____

_____

Based on your numerology, what do you think your purpose is?

_____

_____

_____

_____

_____

_____

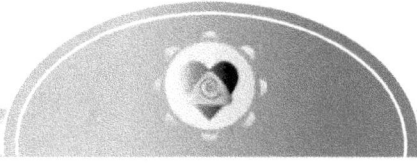

Your Astrological Life Purpose

"Astrology opens to us a book of universal pictures. Each picture is born of order and meaning. Every astrological birth-chart is a signature of the cosmos—or of God . . . Life is a process, and every process is cyclic." (pp. 19–20)

~ Dane Rudhyar
The Pulse of Life: New Dynamics in Astrology

Note: The more input from the different sites, the more clarity. Try them all for many different perspectives!

- Go to www.alabe.com for your free astrology chart. You want to get your natal or birth chart. What does your astrology chart point you toward as your purpose?

  _____

  _____

- Go to www.antiscia.com for your free astrology chart. This site will give you a more comprehensive astrological view. What do you think is your purpose based on your astrology chart? _____

  _____

  _____

- Google "free Chinese astrology chart," then find a site whose perspective you like and obtain a Chinese or Vedic natal chart. What life purpose does it suggest to you?

  _____

  _____

What common themes do you see about your life purpose?

_____

_____

_____

_____

Exercise #5

Your Astrological Element & Energy Life Purpose

"There are millions and millions of men and women who are discontented, depressed, and unhappy square pegs in round holes (or round pegs in square holes), whose talents, abilities and 'daydreams' (in reality, the wise urgings of the Higher Self) are sadly mismatched with the way they earn their daily bread. It's not only a deplorable waste of manpower and womanpower, but it's a tragic waste of human happiness and joy, which are the birthright of every individual on Earth." (p. 2)

~ Linda Goodman, *Star Signs*

This is Linda Goodman's distillation of the Star Signs and her interpretation of the purpose of each sign. Use your Sun Sign and its qualities for this exercise. How would you like to express them?

_____

_____

_____

_____

YOUR SUN SIGN	ENERGY	PURPOSE
Aries ~ Leader with Fire	Leader who loves attention	Pioneer, loves to start things
Taurus ~ Organizer with Earth	Organizes the facts	Structures empires and deals
Gemini ~ Communicator with Air	Communicates with diversity	Loves mental chess, variety
Cancer ~ Leader with Water	Leader who loves the flow	Imagination, arts, education
Leo ~ Organizer with Fire	Organizes and inspires events	Knows how things should be done
Virgo ~ Communicator with Earth	Communicates practical ideas	Clear thinking, creates order
Libra ~ Leader with Air	Leader keeps things moving	Intellectual, mental, fairness
Scorpio ~ Organizer with Water	Organizes intuitive insights	Independent, unseen guidance
Sagittarius ~ Communicator with Fire	Communicates idealism, excites	Loves challenges and idealism
Capricorn ~ Leader with Earth	Leader creates solid growth	Practical, builds foundations
Aquarius ~ Organizer with Air	Organizes life using intellect	Uses concentration and curiosity
Pisces ~ Communicator with Water	Communicates change, flexible	Counselor, loves multiple layers

Exercise #6
Your Elemental Force Life Purpose

"The mastery of each element presents a different problem to the spirit of man, a problem which—with its three phases—is designed eventually to call forth the divine attributes of Wisdom, Love and Power, and to enable these to manifest through every aspect of being." (p. 29)

"We can discover which of these four lessons we have to learn in our present incarnation by studying the sign of the zodiac in which the sun was placed at the time of our birth." (p. 31)

~ Joan Hodgson, *Reincarnation through the Zodiac*

Which sun sign and element are you? Use the previous astrology exercises to find this answer. My sun sign is _____. Its element is _____.

"FIRE teaches the lesson of love, its power, mystery and magic. Souls learning to master this element will encounter many experiences designed to show them the true meaning of love ...

"EARTH is concerned with helping the spirit to gain mastery over physical matter, and it teaches the practical lesson of service. Those who return to earth to learn this lesson may often appear absorbed in material life and have no time for spiritual aspirations ...

"AIR, the element through which the quickening sunlight and the refreshing rain succor the earth, teaches us the lesson of brotherhood. Of all the four, Air is the most subtle element and best blends and harmonises with the others ...

"WATER teaches us control of the emotions, so that we can find peace ..." (pp. 29–31)

I would add that water also teaches us how to flow through life and release our fears so we can live in harmony with ourselves and life.

How is your "elemental" purpose manifesting in your life?

_____

_____

How would you like to express this elemental purpose meaningfully?

_____

_____

Your Psychological Purpose

Practical & Psychological Aspects of Who You Are

- *Personality*
- *Aptitudes*
- *Practical & Preferred Talents*
- *Life Retrospectives*
- *Themes of Meaning*
- *Your Genius*

Practical & Psychological Aspects of Who You Are

This section will help you explore and articulate all the 3D things you enjoy and do well—things you have an aptitude for or that you just naturally do with ease. Each of these tools helps you to express your purpose.

Psychological Assessments

Psychological aspects of yourself can be assessed through theMyers-Briggs or Jungian type testing. Another useful psychological assessment, which was perfected by the Sufis millennia ago, is the Enneagram. This assessment is predicated on your personal surroundings—family, lifestyle, level of existence, family structure, placement, and so on. It shows the personality structure you create to respond to your circumstances and stimuli in ways that help you develop coping strategies to survive and thrive. These tools show you practical and spiritual ways to express your gifts and purpose. The assessments will give you an idea of how "nature and nurture" have commingled in your personality and life. They will provide and create patterns that allow you to develop the organization necessary to be fulfilled and successful in your life. They offer ways of deciphering your personality to determine your preferences and purpose that are really important to you.

A Retrospective Review of Your Life

The majority of this section offers exercises of reflection on your childhood interests, your preferences, and the particular things that have had significant meaning to you throughout your life. Try out some of the retrospective exercises for a more expansive look at your life; this can also include the exercises on what has meaning for you. *Don't dismiss anything about yourself in this process.* Look at your life objectively and note what it is that you can do, even if you are not currently doing anything with it.

Remember, everything you do, consciously or not, is in some way preparing you to express your purpose or the expression of your purpose, which uses the best you of who you are and what you have to offer to make it happen. You will see from these exercises that your purpose is or can be expressed in your profession.

Your Personality Type's Life Purpose

"There are several Jungian Typology testing websites for people to discover their personality types and preferences. Each test strives to show you how you best function in life."

~ Suzanne Strisower

Here are several different sites that offer the same kind of test. Check them out and do the one that feels most aligned with you. Write down your answers below.

⬦ Go to www.humanmetrics.com for your free Jungian Typology test. Do the assessment and learn about your type. _____

_____

⬦ Go to www.keirsey.com for your free Jungian Typology test. Do the assessment and learn more about your type. _____

_____

⬦ Go to www.typelogic.com for your free Jungian Typology test. Do the assessment and learn more about your type.

_____

_____

What do you think your purpose is, based on your type?

_____

_____

Based on your type, what would you like to do that could be a better and more meaningful expression of your purpose? _____

_____

_____

EXERCISE #8

Your Archetype's Life Purpose

"Each of the archetypes carries with it a worldview, and with that different life goals and theories about what gives life meaning. Orphans seek safety and fear exploitation and abandonment. Martyrs want to be good, and see the world as a conflict between good (care and responsibility) and bad (selfishness and exploitation). Wanderers want independence and fear conformity. Warriors strive to be strong, to have an impact upon the world, and to avoid ineffectiveness and passivity. Magicians aim to be true to their inner wisdom and to be in balance with the energies of the universe. Conversely, they try to avoid the inauthentic and the superficial.

"Each archetype projects its own learning task onto the world. People governed by an archetype will see its goal as ennobling and its worst fear as the root of all the world's problems." (pp. 4–5)

~ Carol Pearson, *The Hero Within*

Circle the column that most applies to you. Then journal about how this is most important and purposeful to you or the life you would like.

ARCHETYPES	ORPHAN	MARTYR	WANDERER	WARRIOR	MAGICIAN
Intellect/ Education Style	Wants authority to give answers	Learns or foregoes learning to help others	Explores new ideas in own way	Learns through competition, achievement	Allows curiosity, learns in group or alone, it's fun
Work	Wants an easy life, would rather not work	Sees as hard and unpleasant, but necessary	"I'll do it myself." Seeks vocation	Works hard for a goal and expects a reward	Works at true vocations, sees work as its own reward
Material World	Feels poor, wants to win the lottery, inherit money	Believes that it is more blessed to give than to receive	Becomes a self-made person, may sacrifice money for independence	Works hard to succeed, makes system work for self, prefers to be rich	Feels prosperous with a little or a lot, has faith will always have necessities, doesn't hoard
Task/ Achievement	Overcoming denial, hope innocence	Ability to care, to give up, and give away	Autonomy, identity, vocation	Assertiveness, confidence, courage, respect	Joy, abundance, acceptance, faith

(Archetype chart taken from pages 20–21)

EXERCISE #9

Your Enneagram's Life Purpose

"Who are these people around me? What do they want or need from me? Why do they do or say those things? How can I understand them? How can I understand myself? Why do I long for and work for something with all my heart and then, in a momentary flash, do the very same thing that will destroy my chances of getting it?

"Some years ago, after having worked in the area of personal growth and spirituality for a combined total of over 30 years, we were introduced to a secret wisdom known as the Enneagram. It is purported to be over 4,000 years old and intertwined in the bases of many of the world's major religions. It was said of the Enneagram that it not only held solutions to the questions we have just raised, it also answered the even more significant questions lying dormant within the depths of the unconscious mind." (pp. 1–2)

~ Kathleen Hurley & Theodore Dobson, *What's My Type?*

Go to one of the free Enneagram websites and take an assessment to learn about your "type" and your "wings." Here are some sites: http://www.similarminds.com (This assessment is quick.) http://www.eclecticenergies.com (This assessment shows the Enneagram's depth.) Pick one or both and take their tests.

I understand my type to be: _____

_____

My underlying motivations and desires are: _____

_____

My purpose in doing or being this type now is to: _____

_____

I can see how I am expressing my purpose in my life by:

_____

_____

_____

_____

Your Cultural Creative's Life Purpose

"What makes the appearance of the Cultural Creatives especially timely today is that our civilization is in the midst of epochal change, caught between globalization, accelerating technologies and a deteriorating planetary ecology. A creative minority can have enormous leverage to carry us into a new renaissance instead of a disastrous fall."

~ Paul Ray and Sherry Anderson, *The Cultural Creatives: How 50 Million People Are Changing the World*

What are your values, and how do you want to make a difference? Circle all that apply.

Values of the Cultural Creatives and Their Expression

1. **Global Concerns** – social justice and environmental sustainability
2. **Nature** – love Nature and concerned about its conservation and preservation
3. **Environment** – do what is necessary to save it by buying products with small footprint and long useful life cycle
4. **Political Spectrum** – want authentic, action-oriented, triple bottom line, sustainable officials and candidates
5. **Corporate Conscience** – want corporations to be good citizens and stewards of the community and environment
6. **Equality for All People** – particularly for women and minorities in the workplace and homes around the world
7. **Nonviolence** – want disagreements worked out peaceably and without violence, regardless of the scale of conflict
8. **Education** – funding for children to become inspired members of society and contribute to the global community
9. **Lust for Learning** – Life is an adventure to be explored and fully experienced in all ways: mentally, emotionally, physically, spiritually, and globally in whatever learning tracks or treks are desired
10. **Financially Responsibility** – living within one's means, disdain for greed
11. **Personal Development** – self-directed, focused on psychological and spiritual development
12. **Will/Desire to Create** – a better quality of life for the planet, self-expression gives life meaning
13. **Optimism** – know the inherent goodness of humanity and the power to effectuate positive change
14. **Success** – in terms of fulfillment: personal satisfaction, meaning, and making a difference, not solely focused on amassing a fortune
15. **Spiritual Life** – know there is something bigger than ourselves, focused on divine forces and the Great Mystery
16. **Relationships** – conscious/co-creative, equal partnerships that are dynamic and authentic
17. **Mentoring** – help other people, bring out the best in themselves and giving back to the community
18. **Volunteering** – give time/energy and resources to causes they are committed to

What issue(s) are most important to you? Write down the ways you have a commitment, dedication or purpose to fulfill in any of these areas.

_____

_____

_____

EXERCISE #11

Your "Who Am I" Life Purpose

"There are four simple questions to ask yourself . . .

"WHO AM I? Beneath all of the stories of our past, beneath the joys and sorrows, we have an essential nature that is whole and unbroken. What is this true nature, and how do we find it?

"WHAT DO I LOVE? By what star do we navigate our journey on the earth? What we love will shape our days and provide the texture for our inner and outer life. How can we plant what we love in the garden of life?

"HOW SHALL I LIVE, KNOWING I WILL DIE? Every moment in life is a precious gift. In our brief time here, what qualities do we wish to cultivate? If we are aware of our mortality, we can live less by accident and live instead with clarity and purpose.

"WHAT IS MY GIFT TO THE FAMILY OF EARTH? Each of us has a gift to bring to the table, and the family of the earth yearns to receive it. How do we uncover our true gift?" (p. xii)

~ Wayne Muller, *How Then Shall We Live?*
Four Simple Questions That Reveal the Beauty and Meaning of Our Lives

Describe your essential qualities and characteristics. What qualities are always with you, no matter what (for example, joy, optimism, hope)? _____

_____

What do you love doing just because you do and WHY?

_____

What qualities do you want to have more of in your life?

_____

How is it that you can always be counted on to contribute to making this life and planet a better place?

_____

_____

Exercise #12

Your Infinite Possibility's Life Purpose

"Welcome, Little One, to Planet Earth.

"If we were speaking to you on your first day of physical experience, we would have said to you: Welcome, Little One, to Planet Earth. There is nothing you cannot be, do, or have. You are a magnificent creator, and you are here by your powerful and deliberate desire to be here. You have specifically applied the wondrous law of Deliberate Creation, and by your ability to do that you are here.

"Go forth and attract life experience to help you decide what you want. And once you have decided, give thought only to that." (p. 162)

~ Esther and Jerry Hicks, *Ask and It Is Given*

Imagine what you can create from a place of Deliberate Creation . . .

What do you want to BE? _____

What do you want to DO? _____

What do you want to HAVE? _____

Write down a short list for each of the following:

* I want to _____

* I most want it (from list above) because _____

_____

* I want to feel excited about what I'm doing because _____

_____

* I want to feel a stronger sense of purpose from what I be, do or have because I

_____

What is the underlying thing you want to experience?

_____

_____

EXERCISE #13
Your Fascination's Life Purpose

"How many times have you become fascinated by something—an animal, a building, a car, a work of art, a fresh breeze—and found that the people around you weren't that fascinated at all? That's because you were born with special senses for everything you enjoy. What you'll be happiest doing is built into your nature, like flying is built into a bird's. That's why talents are called 'gifts.' They're presents you've been given by nature. Living a life you will love means using as many of those gifts as you can find time for, and using the most important ones to the limit. So what do you love?" (pp. 99–100)

~ Barbara Sher, *Live the Life You Love: In Ten Easy Step-by-Step Lessons*

Part 1: Looking at your childhood, your adolescence, and your adulthood, write down the things from each period that you loved or were fascinated by in.

Childhood: _____

Adolescence: _____

Adulthood: _____

Part 2: Now ask yourself what it was about each activity that you most enjoyed and why.

Childhood: _____

Adolescence: _____

Adulthood: _____

Part 3: What are the underlying themes that repeat throughout your life? (These "themes" reflect your Life Purpose.)

_____

_____

_____

_____

Your God's Eye View Life Purpose

"Let your business lead you.

Let it guide you to choose places in your heart you have yet to discover.

Let it call your soul to be fully expressed and engaged in the world.

Let it be the way for you to contribute your unique gifts to the world.

Let it be your tool for making the planet a better place.

Let it be your vehicle for leaving a legacy long after you are gone.

Let it be YOU . . . mind and body, heart and soul." (p. 10)

~ Christine Kloser, *The Freedom Formula*

Christine developed a four-step process of taking a "God's Eye View of Your Life." Look at your life as if from the view of the Divine looking down on you.

Step 1: *Reminisce on Your Past Experiences,* both good and bad. Who has God, Higher Power, or your own personal diety helped you become? What strengths, insights, and commitments do you have as a result of your past?

_____

Step 2: *Look at Your Present Life - Successes, Dreams and Challenges.* What is God trying to tell you in this moment?

_____

Step 3: *A View of the Future.* What do you imagine and envision for yourself in God's perfectly unfolding plan? _____

_____

Step 4: *God's Gift and Vision for You.* Let that communication unfold from a meditative space. Here's a meditation she offers to help with the process: www.TheFreedomFormula. com/Guide

_____

_____

Your Emotional Well-Being's Life Purpose

"On a practical level, thoughts are a major source of anxiety, guilt, fear and sadness—
emotions that probably obstruct healing and certainly cause us a great deal of anguish. It
is not possible to stop thought . . . but it is possible to disengage attention from thought.
One way to do that is to focus instead on sensations from the body. There is great
advantage to having bodies, according to Buddhist teaching, because they are anchored
in the here and now while our minds are careering about the past and future." (p. 197)

~ Andrew Weil, *Spontaneous Healing*

First, let's look at what your emotions want (this helps you know how your energy may
be stuck on specific things). What are you feeling anxious about?

_____

What things do you feel guilty about?

_____

Where or how do you feel fear?

_____

What causes you to feel sadness?

_____

What are the general causes of "negative" emotions or energy in you?

_____

Now, just sit quietly and let your awareness flow through your body and breath. What
does your awareness tell you? See where it is primarily located in your body. Notice
what "message" it has for you. What purpose does it have for getting your attention?

_____

_____

_____

Your Essence's Life Purpose

"Essence is the promise. Essence is the life. Essence is the fulfillment of all our deeper longings. Essence is the answer to all our fundamental questions, absolutely—with no exceptions." (p. 115)

~ A. H. Almaas, *Diamond Heart, Book One: Elements of the Real in Man*

If you didn't fear anything and had total freedom, what would you naturally and instinctively be doing?

_____

If you could just immerse yourself in love, both with yourself and all life, what would that experience feel like to you? Where would you naturally find yourself?

_____

If you could be completely objective with yourself, what would you know about what you came here to do?

_____

What are the things you see others doing that most impact you?

_____

What would be your unique expression of those experiences that you would want to do in the world?

_____

Taking into account all your answers above, what is the universal purpose you incarnated to do?

_____

_____

_____

Your Unexpressed Life's Life Purpose

When I attain to utter forth in verse
Some inward thought, my soul throbs audibly
Along my pulses, yearning to be free
And something farther, fuller, higher ... (p. 55)

Elizabeth Barrett Browning

~ Peg Streep, Editor
An Awakened Spirit: Meditations by Women for Women

Sit quietly with yourself until you feel like expressing the unexpressed. What wants to be verbalized by you about your life? What censored thing yearns to be free? Give voice to it now. Write down the exact words that want to be spoken.

_____

_____

What are the things that would make your soul throb?

_____

What things would make your heart speed up with excitement?

_____

What would take you farther than your wildest dreams?

_____

What would take you beyond your wildest imaginings?

_____

_____

What about your work is significant or makes a difference? How is it in service to something bigger than yourself?

_____

EXERCISE #18

Your Unique Gift's Life Purpose

"You have been uniquely gifted with a specific combination of aptitudes and a predisposition to special interests and emotions. These are your strengths and values ... Connecting with your purpose does not have to turn your world on its ear. It does not require massive sacrifice or suffering. It simply requires a shift in your perspective, recognition for what has always been within you, and a willingness to offer those gifts in service." (pp. 100–101)

~ Kimberly Fulcher, *Remodel Your Reality: Seven Steps to Rebalance Your Life & Reclaim Your Passion*

Kimberly poses this series of questions to help you identify what you are a "natural" at and what your passion as purpose might be:

What qualities/aptitudes do you respect and admire about yourself?

_____

What characteristics or qualities do others praise you for?

_____

What things do you gravitate toward online, in books, or as your primary interest?

_____

What kinds of activities or pastimes do you most like doing?

_____

What do you feel most natural doing?

_____

What topic(s) would you love to teach about?

_____

What brings you joy? _____

What do you want to do in service? _____

_____

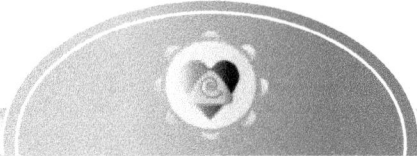

EXERCISE #19

Your Awakened Will's Life Purpose

"When we have moments in which transpersonal will awakens, the accompanying revelation will always require an application. The Real Will reveals solutions, but then the solutions must be lived in three-dimensional expression. If we have not worked to develop adolescent/strong/negating will and skillful/redeeming/nurturant will as well as empowering will, then the insights, solutions, and possibilities uncovered by the transpersonal will shall not truly benefit us. It is an irony of the spiritual path. We must work hard to achieve something and then be prepared to surrender it. Many times it will be given back to us, but always we must be ready to surrender it again." (p. 135)

~ Mark Thurston
Discovering Your Soul's Purpose

There are four stages of development in which your will or purpose is expressed. What has your will focused on?

Stage 1: What did you have an insatiable interest in as a child that you always gravitated toward? _____

_____

Stage 2: Being self-reflective, how do you want to express your individuality apart from what you've known up to this point and are comfortable doing?

_____

Stage 3: The "awakened will" can appear through lucid dreams or super-real experiences. What has been revealed to you? _____

_____

Stage 4: While meditating, what have you experienced of your transpersonal will or "Soul Self?" _____

_____

_____

Your Search for Meaning's Life Purpose

"The greatest task for any person is to find meaning in his or her life. Frankl saw three possible sources for meaning: in work (doing something significant), in love (caring for another person), and in courage during difficult times." (p. X/Foreword)

~ Harold S. Kushner, (Foreword), Viktor E. Frankl
Man's Search for Meaning

Each of these three sources of meaning is an expression of your purpose. Contemplate yours. What shows up for you? Write down your responses, thoughts, and insights.

What about your work is significant or makes a difference?

_____

_____

How is your work in service to something bigger than yourself?

_____

_____

How has being in love or caring for another person brought meaning and purpose to your life? _____

_____

_____

_____

During difficult times, what have you committed your life energy to? What are you wanting to happen so things on the planet can be different?

_____

_____

_____

_____

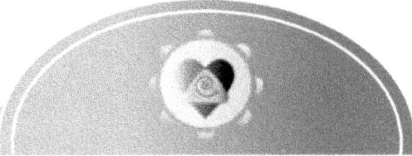

Your Meaningful Activities Life Purpose

"Engaging in meaningful activities promotes bliss. Activities that provide meaning do so by engaging your values, what you feel is important. When your activities are important, you're doing something that makes a difference. You are infused with a sense of purpose, which lifts you above the mundane and the dreary." (p. 73)

~ Beverly Potter, *Finding a Path with a Heart:*
How to Go From Burnout to Bliss

What activities that you engage in do you consider meaningful?

_____

_____

What activities do you do that are important to you and why? (List at least five activities and each one's reason, or your "why.")

_____

_____

_____

_____

_____

What underlying themes keep repeating through your activities and actions? (These themes reflect your Purpose.)

_____

_____

_____

_____

_____

_____

Your Genius Life Purpose

"As I got older, rich dad explained that we all had a genie in us. He said 'The word genius is made up of the words Genie-In-Us. We all have one.'" (p. W-2)

~ Robert Kiyosaki, *Teach to Be Rich:*
Awaken Your Financial Genius

In *Teach to Be Rich,* Robert Kiyosaki offers a five-step process titled "How to Find Your Genius":

1. Find an environment where your genius can come out. What environments support you being your best self?

   _____

   _____

2. Start trusting what your heart says more than what your mind says. What conflicts do you have between your passions being expressed and what your mind feels is "right?"

   _____

   _____

3. Never let your shortcomings, lack of knowledge, lack of resources, fear, or incompetence stop you. What do you back away from that you really want to be doing? _____

   _____

4. Have the courage to find your way of getting things done. Left to your own devices and free of criticism, how would you like to move forward? _____

   _____

5. Have faith in your higher knowledge and trust your intuition. What are your divine wisdom and intuition telling you to do?_____

   _____

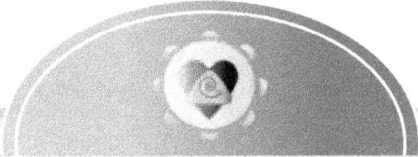

Your New Reality Life Purpose

"While you are here on Earth, you are contributing who you are—your thoughts, your dreams, and your passion for life—into an atmosphere of a global mind that is hungry for, more than anything else, spiritual light." (p. 135)

"Remember, every creative genius in history was a person pursuing the activity they loved most . . . Right action springs from within, from your spiritual heart or inner self . . . When you follow your heart, you express your inner joy through meaningful service to humanity." (pp. 154–155)

~ Owen Waters, *The Shift*

Owen Waters' Nine-Point New Reality Plan

1. LEARNING: What do you have a curiosity to know that would empower you?

_____

2. HEALTH: What motivates and empowers you to be more active in your life? What things would create aliveness for you? _____

3. SKILLS: What skills or talents would you like to develop that you would enjoy doing? _____

4. CONNECTION: How would you like to be more connected with your own heart? What messages have you received three or more times? _____

_____

5. MEDITATION: Ask your Self for guidance to open up the space for you to know or see your path unfolding. What symbols show up for you during meditation?

_____

6. JOY: What gives you the experience of joy? _____

7. CREATIVITY: Using your skills and creativity, what do you want to create?

_____

8. GRATITUDE: What are you most grateful for? _____

9. SERVICE: What do you love doing most? _____

_____

Exercise #24

Your Mission and Calling's Life Purpose

"Mission, vision, vocation, calling, bliss, meaning, passion, these are just some of the words that convey our human need to identify and express purpose. Ultimately, finding your purpose is a spiritual quest. It represents your ability to connect with something greater than yourself." (p. 15)

~ Jim White, *What's My Purpose?*

Contemplate the quotation above. Then write down the first thing that comes to your mind to complete each sentence:

* My mission in life is _____

* The vision I have for my life is _____

  _____

* The vocation that is most fulfilling to me is _____

  _____

* What do these three things have in common? _____

  _____

* My calling is _____

* What is it that gives me bliss and fulfillment _____

  _____

* What is it that gives my life meaning and purpose _____

  _____

* I have a passion for _____

What is the underlying theme—the "something bigger"—you are serving?

_____

_____

_____

EXERCISE #25
Your Wizard's Life Purpose

"What no rational scholar will tell you is that people who see life backward may actually perceive it more accurately than anyone else. You won't read in academic journals that the words 'wizard' and 'wisdom' come from the same root, because the backward-living contrarian often sees magical truths unavailable to people who can only look forward . . . But I've found that the contrarian instinct, the 'wrong' reaction, the socially unacceptable statement is often the seed of destiny struggling to germinate. If you remember feeling painfully unacceptable, especially during your youth, you might want to explore those memories for truths your subsequent socialization thrashed out of you." (p. 14)

~ Martha Beck, *Steering by Starlight*

What did you have a passion to do or experience as a child, but didn't or couldn't due to the circumstances you found yourself in? What was it you wanted to experience?

_____

_____

_____

What regrets or things would you still like to experience? _____

_____

_____

What was the interest or vocation you wanted to pursue that others found unacceptable, so you didn't pursue it? _____

_____

Using hindsight, what course correction would you like to make so your life more accurately reflects who you truly are? _____

_____

_____

_____

EXERCISE #26
Your Body/Mind/Being Life Purpose

"The biological process of the hierarchic organization of organ systems constituting a body (soma); there is the psychic process organizing individual experience by ego synthesis (psyche); and there is the communal process of the cultural organization of the interdependence of persons (ethos).

"To begin with, each of these processes has its own specialized methods of investigation that must, in fact, stay clear of each other in order to isolate and study certain elements basic to nature and to man. But, in the end, all three approaches are necessary for the clarification of any intact human event." (pp. 25–26)

~ Erik Erikson, *The Life Cycle Completed*

This quotation provides a great opportunity to look at your life through the three different lenses—your body, your psyche, and how you relate to others and the whole. Spend thirty minutes with this exercise, pondering without any limitations what you would do if you could do anything—with your body, with your being, and for the community. What would you do in each of those ways?

⬦ My body wants to: _____

_____

⬦ My mind wants to: _____

_____

⬦ My being wants to experience for its own sake: _____

_____

⬦ The thing I would love most love to do with people, humanity, and/or the collective:

_____

Now, look inside these three responses. What do they have in common? What is the WHY? _____

_____

_____

Your Life Purpose Mandala

"No matter their form, mandalas offer us a profound way to examine our inner reality, to integrate that understanding with our physical selves, and to feel connected to the greater universe." (p. 1; image p. 245)

~ Susanne F. Fincher, *The Mandala Workbook*

Use this mandala to visually illustrate your purpose. Write the external manifestations of your purpose on the rays of the sun. Write the internal qualities that you feel on the waves. Write your purpose in the sun as your vision to follow. Perhaps add your face above the hands to personalize it. Complete and celebrate yourself and your purpose made visible!

SECTION 4

Your Professional Purpose

Your Skills, Gifts, Expertise, & Career

- *Career & Work Preferences*
- *Gifts & Talents*
- *Special Interests*
- *Ways of Service*

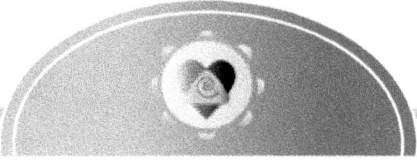

Your Skills, Gifts, Expertise, & Career

At the present time, the terms *profession* and *career* are intertwined. They should be separated to more accurately reflect their meanings. According to *Webster's Encyclopedic Unabridged Dictionary*, *profession* means "things that we have expertise in and do," whereas *career* refers to "the body of our life's work and its accomplishments." A career is far more encompassing than a profession; it utilizes our professional skills to accomplish something.

Your Professional Skills & Career Preferences

This section is designed for you to think about yourself professionally, starting with your expertise, skill set, and preferences. Then you'll take a macro, more comprehensive look at your career—your cumulative professional endeavors, which are the things you have accomplished. Finally, you'll explore your future vision of possibility for yourself. This understanding will give you another perspective on your underlying reason or purpose.

Your External Accomplishments & Feedback

The exercises in this section include a continuum from professional endeavors to your career accomplishments. They ask you to identify whether you are introverted or extroverted, get input from your friends or peers about what they perceive as your accomplishments, consider your own accomplishments by imagining yourself as a CEO, describe your visions for future possibilities you'd like to create, identify how you would give back, explore your ministry, and much more. Choose exercises that provide you the most value, not the ones you find easy to do or the most comfortable. I recommend doing Your Friends' View of Your Life Purpose, Your Serving and Giving Life Purpose, Your Achievements' Life Purpose, and Your Inner CEO's Life Purpose as starting points. The last exercises refer to giving back and your personal ministry.

This section is sequential—it should be more concrete and start to give you a definitive sense, from a career perspective, of what your professional energies are consistently drawn or directed toward. The focus or direction that keeps revealing itself is your Life Purpose. Remember, your job is to be clear, not modest, in your answers in this section for the best results!

Your Personality's Life Purpose

"Personality type also shows us how individuals prefer to orient themselves to and deal with the world around them . . . Understanding your personality type provides a useful tool to help us choose satisfying work activities and environments." (p. 9)

~ Donna Dunning, *What's Your Type of Career?*
Unlock the Secrets of Your Personality to Find Your Perfect Career Path

According to Dunning, there are eight natural ways of working, which can be broken down into two categories: *introverted* and *extroverted.* Of the eight types below, which one do you fit into? Circle the one that feels most "natural" and reflects who you are.

4 EXTROVERTED Types (prefer to interact with the world around them):

- RESPONDERS: Act and Adapt ~ immediately react to their environment and see the problems and opportunities present

- EXPLORERS: Innovate and Initiate ~ scan the environment for patterns and ideas to create what could be

- EXPEDITERS: Direct and Decide ~ like to be in charge and solve complex problems efficiently

- CONTRIBUTORS: Communicate and Cooperate ~ appreciate others and use relationships to organize and create events, processes, and activities that are harmonious

4 INTROVERTED Types (like to think things through for themselves):

- ASSIMILATORS: Specialize and Stabilize ~ integrate detailed facts and information from the past before making decisions and taking action

- VISIONARIES: Interpret and Implement ~ use data, ideas, and experiences to create possibilities for changing systems or processes for the future

- ANALYZERS: Examine and Evaluate ~ logically look at a situation and ask themselves questions to create the best course of action

- ENHANCERS: Care and Connect ~ focus on how others feel to evaluate situations and circumstances and relate them to personal and human values

Which type are you? _____

How can the qualities of your type help you express your purpose in life?

_____

EXERCISE #29
Your Work's Life Purpose

"Work becomes a way of giving of himself. His work (perhaps because of the way in which I am using it here, the term 'vocation' is a more accurate word) provides him with a way of dedicating himself to life. Through it, or—if he is retired or if he doesn't work in the formal sense—through his hobbies and community involvements, he cultivates his talents, stands in for others, exhibits his involvement and connection to the world. Through his work this individual at the same time both loses himself yet becomes more distinctive.

"It is this radical transformation of duty into love, fascination or pleasure which allows the individual to feel that he is at play . . . And because he has fully committed his heart, attention and intention to doing the work (and doing it with a kind of narrowed, intense focus which transcends ordinary consciousness) he heightens his energies and intelligence, thus is able to give his all to the job at hand." (p. 177)

~ Marsha Sinetar, *Do What You Love
and the Money Will Follow*

In what ways do you love to "throw" yourself into life? _____

_____

What work, hobbies, or community involvement are you currently actively and passionately involved in? _____

_____

What activities do you lose yourself in?

_____

What gives you the greatest satisfaction, whether or not it's for money? _____

_____

What do you most love to do? _____

_____

_____

Exercise #30

Your Personal Life Purpose

"The Personal Journey. You are living the life you chose for the specific challenges and opportunities it would afford you. Before you were born, you and your spiritual guides selected a life in which you would be able to work on tendencies that had previously challenged you in other lifetimes or that would further develop your consciousness. Your purpose each moment is to make choices that advance your evolution as a soul." (p. 273)

~ Carol Adrienne
The Purpose of Your Life: Finding Your Place in the World
Using Synchronicity, Intuition and Uncommon Sense

Answer these questions for yourself:

* Who are the people you would love to model your life after (for example, healers, artists, business executives, spiritual people)? _____

_____

* What kind of profession do you prefer (for example, adventuring, teaching, healing, creating, caring, promoting)? _____

_____

* Where do you want to be expressing your career (for example, mountains, farmlands, city, another culture or part of the world)? _____

_____

* What are your specialties that you love doing the most? _____

_____

* What are you renowned for doing? What is your expertise and gift that no one does better than you? _____

_____

_____

_____

_____

Your Significant Service's Life Purpose

"That insight is hidden in the word 'vocation' itself, which is rooted in the Latin for 'voice.' Vocation does not mean a goal that I pursue. It means a calling that I hear. Before I can tell my life what I am to do with it, I must listen to my life telling me who I am. I must listen for the truths and values at the heart of my own identity, not the standards by which I must live—but the standards by which I cannot help but live if I am living my own life." (pp. 4–5)

~ Parker J. Palmer, *Let Your Life Speak: Listening for the Voice of Vocation*

What is your inner "voice" sharing with you?

_____

_____

Do you hear your calling telling you about who you are? Describe what it shares with you about yourself.

_____

_____

What are your truths and values that give you a passion you desire to express as your purpose in life? _____

_____

_____

How would you ideally like to create a life that will express your true potential—a life based on who you are, your values, and your truth?

_____

_____

_____

_____

Your Achievements' Life Purpose

"Like gold ore, your achievements have to be 'panned' in order to find the nuggets, small and large. Your achievements have to be examined, and la borrasca [amalgam—the ore byproducts] separated from the gold. When you have the golden information, when you know your best self and your best capabilities, you will come to know the goals you want to reach. As each goal is examined, the habit of success becomes more deeply entrenched, and constantly bigger and more enticing goals become attainable." (p. 48)

~ Bernard Haldane
How to Make a Habit of Success

Write down the first achievements that come to mind that you have enjoyed doing, have done well, and made you feel good when they were done. _____

_____

Write down the comments people have made to you over the years that start with "You were born to be or do . . ." _____

_____

List two achievements for each five-year period of your life that brought you the most satisfaction. (Use your journal if needed.)

_____

What were or are the things that you have loved to collect? _____

_____

What do you love to research or explore? _____

_____

Write down the underlying talents you have that have helped you in your achievements.

_____

_____

_____

Your Inner CEO's Life Purpose

"The truth is that you came into this life with a specific life purpose or mission. There's something specific you came here to do, contribute, experience, or learn as a result of your time here. Making those contributions, having those experiences, and learning what you came here to learn is your primary 'job.' It's the journey you came here to take, and it's a very important one." (p. 29)

~ Robert Scheinfeld, *The 11th Element: The Key to Unlocking Your Master Blueprint for Wealth and Success*

Do a visualization to meet your Inner CEO. Quietly imagine yourself in charge of your world or reality. Let your Being guide your visualization to have the experience of being a CEO and get a sense of how powerful you can or could be in life. Another way to think of this is to let yourself daydream about what your life would be like if you were a CEO. Then ask yourself these questions.

What did you discover that you came here to do?

_____

What is your specific mission or Life Purpose that you discovered you are executing?

_____

What have you come here to contribute or experience? _____

_____

According to your Inner CEO, what is the primary lesson or thing that you incarnated to be, do, or have? _____

_____

What is your Inner CEO's name? _____

How have you been guided to connect with your Inner CEO in the future? _____

_____

Describe your Inner CEO: _____

_____

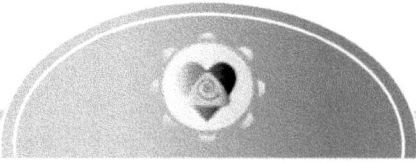

EXERCISE #34

Your Visionary Life Purpose

"Visions are magical. They function in strange ways to guide you to achieving them. When you see the world in terms of explicit objectives, opportunities and options, serendipitous things seem to show up to help you get to where you want to go. You don't have to understand how they work to appreciate that visions really do work." (p. 74)

~ John L. Petersen, *A Vision for 2012*

What future have you visualized for yourself? _____

_____

What visions have you been having? What daydreams, dreams, and so on, have you been having? _____

_____

What objectives, opportunities, or options are you considering that inspire you now?

_____

_____

_____

What visions do you have for the future that you would like to accomplish?

_____

_____

_____

What do you see that all these answers have in common? _____

_____

_____

_____

_____

EXERCISE #35
Your Blissful Life Purpose

"Bliss is the enjoyable feeling of well-being experienced when you're fully involved with what you are doing. There is a sensation of being in harmony with your surroundings. Loss of self, where you feel 'one' with the activity and the moment, is among its most notable characteristics. There is no sense of separation between you and what you are doing." (p. 10)

~ Beverly Potter, *Finding a Path with a Heart:*
How to Go from Burnout to Bliss

Where do you find your bliss? Complete each statement below:

I feel totally immersed and satisfied in my work when I'm doing or being _____

_____

I'm always in the flow when I'm _____

I feel bliss with another person when we're _____

It would make me really happy to buy or have _____

_____

Some meaningful activities that bring me joy include _____

_____

A gut feeling or hunch that I followed that turned out fantastically was _____

_____

What do these things all have in common that create joy and bliss for you?

_____

_____

How might these answers be connected to your Life Purpose? _____

_____

_____

_____

Exercise #36
Your Gift's Life Purpose

"Every day, life offers many moments for us to be more of ourselves—to bless the world with who we are and to be blessed by others—to Show Up. The questions life asks each of us in these moments include 'Are you willing to stand by your own heart?' 'Are you willing to touch life with your essential nature?' 'Are you willing to give the world the gift of your self?" (p. 100)

~ Erica Ross-Krieger, *Seven Sacred Attitudes*

A life coach often asks clients to make inquiries—to ask yourself questions that provide a deeper sense of what's true for you. Here are some inquiries offered by Erica:

◈ What can you feel blooming in you? _____
_____
_____

◈ What are you wanting to grow in your life? _____
_____
_____

◈ What would you like to plant in the garden of your life? _____
_____
_____

◈ What do you want to do or say in the world? _____
_____
_____
_____

◈ What one word or phrase that describes your values would you have printed on a T-shirt? _____
_____

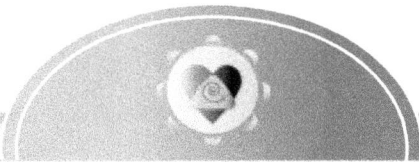

Your Spiritual Ministry's Life Purpose

"Before being called to something, we are called to [be] Someone. Before we are called to do, we are called to be. Our primary calling is to be in a personal relationship with God through faith in Jesus Christ. The Bible tells us that God has called us into fellowship with his son Jesus Christ. God created us and knows our strengths, weaknesses, dreams, and fears." (p. 5)

~ Kevin & Kay Marie Brennfleck, *Live Your Calling*

Live Your Calling offers a list of practical and spiritual gifts. Circle all that you feel called to do. Then, for each gift you circled, fill in the last column with how you express or would like to express the gift. Remember, this is not about what you want to do . . .

SPIRITUAL GIFT	ITS QUALITIES	YOUR EXPRESSION
Administration	Creates goals and accomplishes them	
Discernment	Knows and listens to divine messages	
Evangelism	Passion about sharing message	
Encouragement	Ability to guide and help others	
Faith	Trusts God and overcomes obstacles	
Giving	Ability to give generously	
Helper in service	Accomplishes supportive tasks	
Hospitality	Demonstrates love through comfort	
Intercession	Prayer for long periods of time	
Knowledge	Understands and shares wisdom	
Leadership	Directs others towards future goals	
Mercy	Ministers to people in need	
Pastor	Directs spiritual growth of group	
Teaching	Helps others know and love God	
Wisdom	Applies knowledge to problems	
Apostleship	Starts new schools of thought	
Healing	Ability to heal body-mind-spirit	
Miracles	Prays and creates supernatural acts	
Prophecy	Shares divine message and guidance	

EXERCISE #38
Your God-Ordained Life Purpose

"You were put on earth to make a contribution. You weren't created just to consume resources—to eat, breathe, and take up space. God designed you to make a difference with your life . . . You were created to add to life on earth, not just take from it. God wants you to give something back." (p. 227)

~ Rick Warren, *The Purpose Driven Life*

Which of these five God-ordained purposes from Pastor Rick Warren most reflects what you feel or are called to do? Circle one:

* **Worship** ~ "living your whole life for God's pleasure"
  Are you living your life as an offering to God?

* **Fellowship** ~ "being as committed to each other as we are to Jesus Christ"
  Are you creating spiritual community?

* **Discipleship** ~ "becoming like Jesus Christ"
  Are you living your life embodying his teachings?

* **Ministry** ~ "using your shape to serve others"
  Do you have a personal ministry in which you serve?

* **Mission** ~ "sharing the Good News with others"
  Are you a citizen of the world who goes where you are led?

Write down your God-ordained purpose and how you carry it out now. If this troubles you, pray to God or Jesus and ask for guidance about your path of purpose and service.

_____

_____

_____

_____

_____

_____

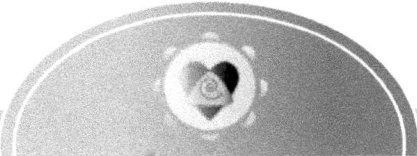

EXERCISE #39

Your Friends' View of Your Life Purpose

"Request meaningful feedback from your family, friends, and professional colleagues about how they experience you. What's special that you take for granted but they are impressed and inspired by? How they see you can guide you toward your purpose and ways to optimize your life professionally."

~ Suzanne Strisower

Choose six people who are willing to share some feedback about their perceptions of your life. Share with them the types from page 66, and ask them which type they think you are. (Don't tell them in advance which one you think you are.) Explain that you want honest feedback, and ask them in what particular ways they see you optimizing those gifts.

Name	Gifts, Qualities & Perceived Type	How You Should Use Them & WHY	Your Life Purpose
Person #1			
Person #2			
Person #3			
Person #4			
Person #5			
Person #6			

Write down their responses in the grid. What is the consensus of their opinions and their feedback? Does it match how you see yourself? How does their input help you better understand your gifts, strengths, and purpose?

Exercise #40

Your Dreamstar Life Purpose

"If an intimate circle (of friends, family, group) wants to interact with each other's dreams and visionary experiences, we recommend a format called 'Dreamstar.' This is a powerful way of exploring the dreaming consciousness [that] works best when the circle has developed at least a modest sense of trust and a willingness to take risks." (p. 77)

~ Jack Zimmerman & Virginia Coyle
The Way of Council

Listen to your dream's visions:

1. Play some meditation or other background music.

2. Sit or lie in a circle with each person's feet facing out of the circle. Relax and get comfortable.

3. Do a relaxation exercise and breathing technique to allow people to access a dream or trance state.

4. Another possible way is to invite your guides and have them act as participants during your sleep.

5. Tell your story of your dream that has arisen to those in the circle. Listen to what you have to say and what others share.

Write down your dream vision for yourself: _____

_____

_____

What details did others contribute to your vision that enhances it? _____

_____

_____

_____

_____

Exercise #41

Your Serving and Giving Life Purpose

"The purpose of life is quite simply to live. The question then becomes, how are we going to live? If, when contemplating your life purpose, you find words and concepts coming to mind such as service, sharing, compassion, loving, empathy, or kindness, you probably will not be truly satisfied until a goodly portion of your life is involved in giving and serving. 'When people are serving' wrote John Gardner, 'life is no longer meaningless.' When we give, at the very least, we are more likely to experience that our life has meaning; that we are living our life on purpose. We sometimes find our lives in losing it in service to others." (p. 5)

~ John-Roger, *Serving and Giving:*
Gateways to Higher Consciousness

Write down ways that you are or would like to be in service:

* I am in service to others by _____

_____

* I am in service to the planet by _____

_____

* I like to share with others by _____

_____

* I show compassion by _____

* I express my loving to and by _____

_____

* I give empathy by _____

* I express kindness by _____

_____

Write down the way you would most love to be of service—in other words, the vision you have in your heart if there were no limitations. _____

_____

SECTION 5
Your Transitional Purpose

Your Next Steps, Midlife, & Beyond

* *Desires You Want to Experience*
* *Midlife Assessments*
* *Unfinished Business*
* *Legacy*
* *Giving Back*

Your Next Steps, Midlife, & Beyond

This section is dedicated to people who are transitioning personally or professionally or who are entering or in the second half of their lives. Each change or transition brings with it the opportunity to reassess one's lives. Each person reaches a certain level of accomplishment or has experienced a major life change that requires a reevaluation of his or her life.

Traditionally, life often takes on a new meaning and purpose at midlife or in times of transition. It is a time to answer questions about what you want to be, do, have, explore, fulfill, or finish. It's a time to look at your next step objectively, whether it is a choice about a career change, retirement, or an encore career. What do you want to do in the next stage of your life or as a legacy before you leave this earthly existence? Your own motivation or purpose is sacred—and both finite and infinite.

Assessment of Your Current Life, Midlife, or Sunset Years Direction & Course

Ideally, at midlife, every person starts a "midlife assessment" process to course-correct so they can experience the fullness of life and be passionate and purposeful about what matters most to them for the rest of their lives. Otherwise, they are likely to experience a "midlife crisis," in which the current reality doesn't match their needs, wants, desires, and purpose for being. This can lead to a desire for a midlife career that better reflects and fulfills the contemporary person.

The transition into an encore career or the "sunset years" can create an urgency and a new sense of purpose to get things in order financially for retirement years or to complete unfinished business.

The exercises in this section offer a multiplicity of perspectives on these transition times. Remember, transitions and midlife are times for course corrections and times to refocus and redirect yourself. Your purpose is an excellent tool to guide you forward or to reconcile you to your current life path.

NOTE: It is important to do these exercises sequentially, as it is most effective to work from the outer, conscious world inward to the subtler parts of yourself. Either way, you will be empowered by your Knowing, Truth, and Choice!

Exercise #42
Your Midlife Phase's Life Purpose

"Four developmental phases shape the way our creative energy grows and the way we express it. Each phase itself is shaped by our chronological age, our history, and our circumstances. And each phase is characterized by changes in how we view and experience life in a combined psychological, emotional, and intellectual sense. I call these 'human potential phases.'

"'Midlife Reevaluation Phase.' During this time creative expression is shaped by a sense of crisis or quest...

"'Liberation Phase.' In this phase, typically occurring in those approaching their sixties to early seventies, creative endeavors are shaped with the added energy of a new degree of personal freedom...

"'Summing-Up Phase.' This phase sees creative expression shaped by a desire to find larger meaning in the story of our lives, and to give in a larger way of the wisdom we have accrued...

"'Encore Phase.' This is a time of advancing age, in which creative expression is shaped by a desire to make a strong, lasting contribution on a personal or community level, to affirm life, take care of unfinished business and celebrate one's own contribution." (pp. 78–79)

~ Gene D. Cohen, *The Creative Age*

Circle the phase are you in. Then answer the following questions.

- What needs to be done now? _____

_____

- What do I need to do to optimize my current phase? _____

_____

- What things can I do to more accurately reflect that phase's purpose in my life?

_____

- What career opportunities or professional endeavors do I want or need to still accomplish? _____

_____

Exercise #43

Your Remembrance's Life Purpose

Sea Grapes

The time will come
when, with elation,
you will greet yourself arriving
at your own door, in your own mirror,
And each will smile at the other's welcome,
And say, sit here. Eat.
You will love again the stranger who was yourself.
Give wine. Give Bread. Give back your heart
To itself, to the stranger who has loved you
All your life, whom you ignored
For another, who knows you by heart.
Take down the love letters from the book shelf,
The photographs, the desperate notes,
Peel your own image from the mirror.
Sit. Feast on your life." (p. 206)

Derek Walcott

~ David Whyte, compiler, *The Heart Aroused*

Have an intimate feast with yourself. Bring out old albums, letters, commen-dations, mementos, things you've loved, and things you've long forgotten. Reacquaint yourself with who you really are and dust off your heart and what's truly important to you. How do all these aspects of your past impact you now? _____

_____

Is there a way you want to honor yourself and who you have been that is reflected through this process? _____

_____

Are there any unfinished things that would like to bring to closure or fruition? (Each of these things then becomes a purpose unto itself.) _____

_____

Exercise #44

Your Transitioning Path's Life Purpose

"The 'New Retirement' is not an ending, it's a new beginning, the start of a new life journey of vastly expanded proportion." (p. 1)

~ Richard P. Johnson, *The New Retirement*

This opportunity to make a "new beginning" can happen at any age, not just retirement. Use this exercise to help you make a conscious and vital transition for yourself. This assessment takes you through every aspect of your life.

1. **Daily Routines** ~ Look at how you spend your time in your daily routines and activities. Are they meaningful and purposeful for you?

2. **Peer & Social Interactions** ~ Reflect on the support, validation, and stimulation you receive from peers, colleagues, and employers. How are you creating stimulating personal and social interactions for yourself now?

3. **Financial Viability** ~ Think about your financial stability and legacy. Are you at a point at which you can be financially comfortable, or do you need to think about an encore career? If you are financially stable, what do you want to create with it? How can you express your purpose through your finances?

4. **Physical Health & Well-Being** ~ Consider your vitality. Are there activities, people, places, or things that you still want to experience? Do you need to make your health a priority? If so, how is the reason for those wants or needs connected to fulfilling some inner purpose?

5. **Relationships** ~ Regarding connections to the people closest to you (family, spouse, friends), are there things you still want to share or convey?

6. **Unfinished or Unresolved Items** ~ Is there "unfinished business" in your life? Are there things you still want to be, do, or have, like a "bucket list" you want to achieve?

7. **Legacy** ~ Is there something you want to do or create while you are still here?

These seven points give you a deeper way to explore each of area of your life.

CAREER ~ How do you want to use your skills to best benefit your own ends? How do you want to fill your time meaningfully and productively? _____

_____

MONEY ~ Do you still need to work for a living? If so, what would you like to do that would be fulfilling and financially rewarding? _____

_____

PRIMARY RELATIONSHIPS ~ What kind of personal or intimate partners would you like? Will you have additional family time and flexibility now to share with them?

_____

PEERS & COLLEAGUES ~ What do you want to do for mental stimulation and social interaction that will provide meaning and purpose to you? _____

_____

GROWTH & DEVELOPMENT ~ What deeper sense of reality do you want to explore and experience? What is most important and meaningful to you personally?

_____

REST & RELAXATION ~ How would you like to nurture yourself and make yourself feel good and special? What activities do you want to do for fun? What do you find most enjoyable and invigorating? _____

_____

HOME & WORK ENVIRONMENTS ~ What would you like to do to enhance your living environments and work spaces? _____

_____

WELL-BEING ~ What needs to happen for you to have a zest for life?

◈ Mentally _____

◈ Emotionally _____

◈ Physically _____

◈ Spiritually _____

At this juncture in your life, what is the majority of your focus or purpose and energy devoted to? What area is your primary focus now?

_____

_____

In looking at each area of your life, how do you want to consciously embrace this transition? Move into your transitions, midlife, or retirement consciously so that the outcomes match your desires. Use this information as a transition tool to minimize stress and unfulfilled expectations and to propel you in a direction of your choosing.

Your Current Needs' Life Purpose

"Nature compels physical and cognitive maturation through early adulthood.
Then the need to earn a place in society kicks in: education, career, family, status,
recognition, and achievement." (p. 107)

~ Marc Freedman, *Encore: Finding Work
That Matters in the Second Half of Life*

Take time to revisit Maslow's Hierarchy of Needs (page 30). Look at how far you've
come in your evolutionary purpose. What are you focused on achieving as your purpose
in life at this time of transition, midlife, or beyond? Circle where you are in your life
now and write down how you are fulfilling those needs for yourself now.

Survival ~ Wanting to Get Your Basic Needs Met

_____

Stability ~ Wanting to Have Things in Order

_____

Social ~ Wanting to Be More Connected with the World

_____

Self-Esteem ~ Knowing Yourself and Your Worth

_____

Refinement ~ Creating Balance and Order for Yourself

_____

Self-Actualization ~ Exploring Yourself from the Inside Out

_____

Self-Realization ~ Experiencing Your Divine Connection

_____

EXERCISE #46
Your Masculine Life Purpose

"For most men, [and some women] then, the movement toward midlife is a process of self insulation. Through work achievement, material affluence, the raising of children, and maintenance of marriage they come to be assured about their capacity to cope with external demands. They take pride in achieving benchmarks, and tend to become more inward and less aware of their own limitations and desires. At either end of this statistical norm are the psychological casualties and the more fortunate or exceptional men, those for whom adult life has meant a growing self awareness, increased acceptance and closeness to others, and a sense of their own competence." (p. 212)

~ Michael Farrell & Stanley Rosenberg
Men at Midlife

Which of these is your present experience?

1. Are you focusing on what's real and on your own personal growth path? If so, where is it taking you? _____

    _____

2. Are you still trying to keep up with the person you used to be? If so, what do you want to do for YOU now? _____

    _____

3. Are you overwhelmed with how your life has turned out and feeling dependent on the significant others in your life? If so, what's next? _____

    _____

4. Are you unhappy with yourself and the world and feeling victimized? If so, how can you shift that situation now? _____

    _____

Where would your competence and self-awareness take you now?

_____

_____

Your Feminine Life Purpose

"There were also important differences between the homemakers and the career women. The homemakers had attempted in early adulthood to make family the central component of their life structures within the framework of a Traditional Marriage Enterprise. In the Mid-Life Transition most of them recognized that their marriage enterprise had been a partial or massive failure and that, whatever its previous value, they wanted a different kind of marriage, family, and life structure in the next season. The career women, in contrast, in early adulthood had attempted to pursue an Anti-Traditional Dream. . . . They came to want a full time career with marriage/family in a satisfactory balance . . . In the Mid-Life Transition the career women asked more strongly, 'What do I want?'" (p. 408)

~ Daniel J. Levinson, *The Seasons of a Woman's Life*

Was your life experience more of a family-oriented homemaker or a career woman? The choice I made was _____

What is your purpose in whatever choice you want to consider at this time in your life?

_____

As a homemaker, I put my passion into my family and that reality. Now, I'd really like to: _____

_____

_____

_____

As a career woman, I am now ready to do these things for myself that express my interests and bring me personal meaning and fulfillment: _____

_____

_____

_____

_____

Your Growing Edge's Life Purpose

"During the Middle Passage it is useful to see how one's successes have also been imprisoning, constrictive to the whole person. Jogging and being active in sports, for instance, can be more than a means of managing stress. They can represent ways to get in touch with the sensate world again after spending a week at a desk. For the person who works manually, the life of the mind may call up the inferior function. At first one feels awkward using the less adapted processes, but in the end the psyche responds by a greater sense of grounded well being. In our culture, one cannot count on the cooperation of employers or even family in this process of balancing one's psyche." (p. 77)

~ James Hollis, *The Middle Passage*

What things do you already do well? _____

_____

What things do you feel awkward trying but really want to do? _____

_____

What things do you want to do or experience that would bring about balance in your Being? _____

_____

What things do you feel you've done well but are burned out by and would like to do differently? _____

_____

What do you feel would challenge and inspire you? _____

_____

What would your purpose be in experiencing those things? _____

_____

_____

EXERCISE #49

Your Career Calling's Life Purpose

"Our vocation is one of our voices. It comes from the same Latin root: vox, 'voice,' or vocare, 'to call.' In our thirties and beyond, we are looking for the work that not only pays the bills but allows us to speak in our own voice. This is the cornerstone of a true calling.

"In the second half, it is common to experience feelings of dissatisfaction, alienation, and emptiness in our work. We feel inexplicably lost or more precisely, abandoned. Abandonment literally means 'to be uncalled,' to be without destiny." (pp. 113–114)

~ Mark Gerzon, Coming Into Our Own:
Understanding the Adult Metamorphosis

First: Tune in to your inner voice and listen to what it is calling you to do or experience. What is it suggesting or asking of you? _____

_____

Second: Is there a part of you that wants to break out or break free of something that is holding you back? _____

_____

Third: Do you have a feeling of abandonment, emptiness, or lack of a destiny?

_____

_____

Fourth: Is there something you could do that you've never done and want to experience? What is it? _____

Fifth: What has particular meaning for you now that you're excited about? These "themes" are your Purpose . . . _____

_____

_____

_____

Exercise #50
Your Midlife Value's Life Purpose

"If we think of life as a series of investments . . . As we start on careers, we usually of necessity focus on making a living. Woody [his client at midlife] did that well. But he realized that his life and growth would not fit into that narrow concept. He shifted his perspective from making a living to making a life. In reassessing his priorities and reorienting his life around them, he has restructured his work to better suit the way he wants to live and grow. He has expanded his work portfolio to include learning and teaching, service to the community, and personal development as well as paid employment . . ." (pp. 104–105)

~ William A. Sadler, *The Third Age: 6 Principles for Growth and Renewal After 40*

Shift your focus from making a living to making a life. What are the priorities and values you want to use going forward in your life? _____

_____

How do you want to invest your life force energy? _____

_____

_____

How do you want to teach and learn? _____

_____

How do you want to be in service to your community? _____

_____

What areas of personal development are of interest to you? _____

_____

How could you blend these professional desires into your career and create a fulfilling life's work? Describe what that life looks like. _____

_____

_____

Exercise #51
Your Fulfilled Dreams Life Purpose

Launching Pad

"What are the talents, gifts, and desires that inspire you? Ask yourself, if I could do anything I wanted, even for free, what do I really love or wish I could do? How bad do you want it? For some you're a CEO who wants to be a teacher or a non-professional who wants to translate foreign language skills into becoming a personal tutor. For others it's taking decorating or home repair skills to a new level. Whatever it is, no matter how inconsequential it may seem to others, it's not to you. It's your dream!" (p. 64)

~ Tim Brolus, *Baby Boomers Almanac*

What inspiration will fulfill your dreams and your purpose?

Artistic ~ What artistic goals do you have? _____
_____

Career ~ What level do you strive to achieve professionally? _____
_____

Education ~ What do you still have a craving to learn? _____
_____

Family ~ What would you like to share or express with your family? _____
_____

Physical ~ What do you want to achieve and accomplish physically? _____
_____

Pleasure ~ What gives you pleasure and enjoyment that you want more of? ___
_____

Public Service ~ How can you better humanity or the planet? _____
_____

Exercise #52

Your Baby Boomer's Life Purpose

"The stages corresponding to the early and middle adult years focus on the establishment of close personal relationships (intimacy vs. isolation), and the passing on to the future of one's creative products (generativity vs. stagnation). In the final stage (ego integrity vs. despair), the individual must resolve conflicted feelings about the past, adapt to the changes associated with the aging process, and come to grips with the inevitability of death." (p. 150)

~ Susan K. Whitbourne & Sherry L. Willis
The Baby Boomers Grow Up

How are you currently experiencing your life? Circle the side of each phrase that applies:

Intimate connections vs. Isolation and loneliness

Creating vs. Stagnating

Peaceful vs. Despairing

How can you enhance your current situation now? _____

_____

_____

What do you want from your close personal relationships now? What is the purpose of those relationships for you now? _____

_____

What legacy of creative endeavors do you want to leave for this planet and for those who are important to you? _____

_____

What has meaning, purpose, and value to you now? What gives you inspiration that you want to follow, explore, or express? _____

_____

_____

_____

Your Conscious Evolution's Life Purpose

"It only remains for me, in bringing this work to a close, to define my opinion on three matters which usually puzzle my readers: a) What place remains for freedom (and hence for the possibility of a setback in the world)? b) What value must be given to spirit (as opposed to matter)? and c) What is the distinction between God and the World in the theory of cosmic involution?" (p. 307)

~ Teilhard de Chardin, *The Phenomenon of Man*

For ten minutes during this retrospective period in your life, contemplate these questions for yourself. Listen to your gut feelings and inner voice as you understand the answers to these questions.

What does "the freedom to be uniquely who you are" mean to you? _____

_____

What value do you give to Spirit? _____

_____

What value do you place on Matter? _____

_____

What is the distinction between God and your worldly self? How can you fuse them together for yourself? _____

_____

_____

Spend the next ten minutes meditating on how Spirit and Matter can work together through you. What are you being summoned to do?

_____

_____

_____

_____

EXERCISE #54
Your Legacy's Life Purpose

"Whatever the form, the purpose of an ethical will (or life review) is to provide a means to pass along a legacy to others and to find meaning in our own life—in other words to help us save and savor the world." (p. 68)

"Every time we hear or reflect on [Martin Luther] King's words, we feel their stunning power, in part because they are an embodied expression of his deepest purpose—coming directly from his soul, translated into heartfelt language, so that every single person in his audience could feel the power of his legacy." (p. 73)

*~ Richard J. Leider, Something to Live For:
Finding Your Way in the Second Half of Your Life*

Write your ethical will—what you want people to know about who you are, what you stood for, what was important to you, what you most valued in your life, what you most cherished, what you wished for others, and so on. Be present and thoughtful during this process.

Here are some elements you might want to include:

- Your personal history or important stories or events, the values that you hope will be carried forward, nonmaterial gifts, an epitaph, and blessings or life lessons that you wish to leave to your family, friends, and the world at large.

- It can be a letter, a memoir, a video, a piece of artwork, or anything that helps convey what you want your authentic legacy to be. Be as creative and audacious as you want—this is your life and your legacy that you are sharing!

- Start with a journal for this exercise so you can get clear about the "nuggets" of what you want to leave.

Your Second Half of Life's Life Purpose

"When the psychological self—the adult imago—is fully constituted and fully realized in the second half of life, a person acquires with it the freedom to expand and deploy the expression of psychic energy in a distinctive and highly creative way. The imago opens new vistas, while it also defines the individual's psychological style. It brings this capacity to the personality because it draws together the most important opposites in the individual psyche—the high and the low, the sacred and the profane, the conscious and the unconscious—into a singular pattern." (p. 107)

~ Murray Stein
Transformation: Emergence of the Self

Now write your own story. Create your own Big-Picture Dream using all the different parts of yourself. Tell the next chapter of the story of your life in an unfettered way. Use all the opposites—the hidden things you don't want to share but you do want to experience. Let your hair down and write that chapter—your transition, midlife, or "sunset" experience. What captivates and calls you now? (Use more paper if you need to. The space here is just to get you started.) _____

_____

_____

_____

_____

_____

_____

_____

_____

_____

_____

_____

Your Passion's Life Purpose

"It all starts with following your passion ... Do you have a passion for nature, the environment, animals, families, students, kids, senior citizens, making a local difference or focusing on some key national issues of our time?" (p. 84)

~ David Mills, *10,000 Days:*
A Call to Arms for the Baby Boom Generation

What area(s) do you have a passion for? (You can refer to the Cultural Creatives list on page 45.) _____

_____

What area has strongly impacted you personally (for example, health issues, the environment, social justice, senior issues)? _____

_____

In what ways do you want to be of service or have a personal mission? _____

_____

If you weren't shy and modest, what would you like to accomplish? _____

_____

In what areas do you have expertise that you could plug into in ways that would be fulfilling to you? _____

_____

What type of legacy would you like to leave? _____

_____

_____

* My specific legacy for my family is: _____

* My specific legacy for my community is: _____

* My specific legacy for humanity or the planet is: _____

Your Altruism's Life Purpose

"Specifically, 'positive spirituality' is not bound by an organized system of beliefs, practices, or doctrines that would be descriptive of religion; nor is it restricted to the personal quest for ultimate understanding that would be characteristic of spirituality." (p. 157)

"Each of these concepts is tied to a specific source of meaning acquired during the course of living. Forgiveness facilitates relationships; altruism establishes purpose; and gratitude is a source of positive emotion." (p. 159)

~ Robert Hill, *Positive Aging*

Your purpose can involve a practical focus and application. Describe each of the elements of your current purpose.

- What things in your life would you like to make right that would give you a sense of purpose? _____

  _____

  _____

  _____

- What altruistic endeavors would you like to undertake? _____

  _____

  _____

  _____

  _____

- What things bring you a sense of gratitude and well-being? _____

  _____

  _____

  _____

  _____

EXERCISE #58
Your Middle Age Metamorphosis Life Purpose

"Consider the chrysalis, caterpillar, and the butterfly: The caterpillar doesn't go into the chrysalis, hang out for awhile, and then emerge the same as [she] or he used to be, only looking a bit more worn. He [she] comes out an entirely different being . . . Entering midlife with the same external focus ensures that this process of transformation will be more challenging and frustrating than it needs to be . . . On the other hand, entering midlife with anticipation and an eye to a whole new world of possibility will ensure the next part of your life won't be a route leading to the end, but rather a pathway to a deeper place than you may have ever imagined. Middle age isn't just a matter of aging. When entered into full bore and fully aware, it is the process and result of true transformation." (pp. 201–202)

~ Susan Schachterle
The Bitch, the Crone and the Harlot

If you could envision your transformation, what would you like to see happen? Give yourself permission to think and feel outside the box and outside your comfort zone for a moment. Imagine yourself as a butterfly flitting from place to place, doing the things that nurture you. What are you doing? _____

_____

_____

_____

_____

You might ask yourself this same question before going to sleep and see what your unconscious dream self has in mind for you. What showed up in your dreams?

_____

_____

_____

_____

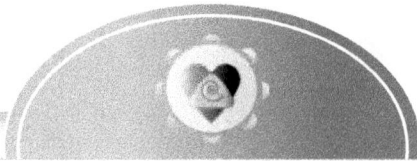

SECTION 6
Your Spiritual Purpose

Your Intuition & Divine Guidance

- *Guided Visualizations*
- *Journeying*
- *Meditations*
- *Hands-On Projects*

Your Intuition & Divine Guidance

In the previous sections, you were asked what you know or have experienced. This section is designed to go beyond your conscious mind with exercises to help you receive guidance from Source through a variety of tools and techniques. Have fun with these; there are no right or wrong answers—only what feels good and right to your Being and Soul.

Exercises Using Intuitive Awareness & Receiving Divine Guidance

This section is comprised of several different types of "spiritual" exercises, including guided visualizations, meditations, and journaling techniques from many different perspectives. Let your Being run wild with you—do these exercises quietly by yourself and let whatever wants to arise from Spirit or the Divine come forth. These exercises are meant to broaden and deepen what has already been revealed to you in the previous sections of the workbook. Some answers may be surprising and very different from what you understood consciously. You will begin to get a more holographic sense of your purpose from the synthesis of all your answers and these new insights from your intuition and the unseen world.

The Guided Visualizations, Past Lives & Meditations

The guided journeys or visualizations (someone talking you into a receptive altered or trance state with the goal of receiving information from your subconscious as well as Divine wisdom) include past lives and possible karmic life purposes. I recommend that you choose ones that you feel most comfortable with.

The meditations invite you to enter a quiet space to receive whatever comes into your awareness from a place of nonjudgmental receptivity. If you are unfamiliar with these techniques, start with visualizations to open up your awareness to be able to receive.

Your Dream Experiences & Journaling Everything

There are specific journaling exercises, but I also recommend that immediately after completing the visualizations, meditations, or dream exercises, you write about what you actually experienced. They can profoundly impact you.

EXERCISE #59
Your Tarot Card's Life Purpose

"The 'Who Am I' Game or 'What Is My Life Purpose?' created by James Wanless, is a great idea and game, which you can play yourself or with others. The goal is to ask the cards, oracle, or your friends to tell you what they see as your Life Purpose. Let them reflect this back to you. This can be done with tarot cards by picking a card for yourself and reading its meaning or by having a friend consciously pick the card that he or she thinks represents you from their perspective. This can be fun and insightful for you and whomever you choose to ask for their input."

~ Suzanne Strisower

If you don't have a tarot deck, go to www.MyDivinationSite.com and ask for your Life Purpose to be revealed. Choose decks that you feel most drawn to and do a one-card reading. If you have your own deck, I recommend pulling a card or finding one that you feel represents your purpose. You can also ask three friends for their insight into your purpose and or do three different online spreads to get a consensus on your purpose.

Pick "your" card and interpret it as your Life Purpose.

Card: _____ Meaning: _____

My Life Purpose Interpretation is: _____

_____

What three cards did others pick for you? Or what three cards did you get online? How do they represent your Life Purpose?

◈ 1st _____

◈ 2nd _____

◈ 3rd _____

The tarot cards show me that my purpose is _____

and I'm supposed to be doing _____

The insights that your friends gave you about your purpose are _____

_____

106

EXERCISE #60

Your Power Animal's Life Purpose

"It is possible to find animals that speak to you in a particular way—the way of power. These creatures may carry special medicine for you, and will call to you in the Dreamtime if you are to study them more closely. Your power ally is a certain species with which you have recognized an important connection. This species becomes your teacher, with whom you allow yourself to grow and learn. Nothing can replace the observation of these creatures in their natural habitats, for this connects you with the Earth, the animal and the Great Mystery." (p. 14)

~ Jamie Sams, *Medicine Cards*

Reflect on your life . . .

What kind of animal has always been there with you?

_____

Which animals fascinate you?

_____

_____

Which qualities of theirs do you most admire and seek to embody?

_____

_____

_____

Check out the symbolism of your power animal in the Native American traditions at: http://www.extrasensory-perceptions-guide.com/power-totem-animal.html. How are you expressing its wisdom?

_____

_____

_____

_____

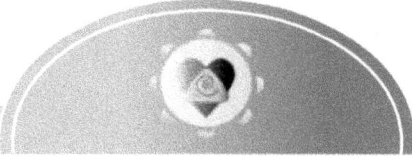

Exercise #61
Your Soul's Lesson's Life Purpose

"As a Divine Immortal Being, the most important aspect of your purpose is to claim and master your creativity. The Earth plane and the human experience offer your soul the best possible classroom in which to discover this, learn through trial and error, and advance in every way. The mystics of your realm referred to this process as alchemy, the process of turning the lead of your ego into the gold of your spirit." (p. 3)

~ Sonia Choquette, *Soul Lessons and Soul Purpose:*
A Channeled Guide to Why You Are Here

Sonia's Soul Lesson #1: Knowing You Are a Divine Immortal Being

It is important to know what level you are operating in so you can most efficiently express your purpose. For instance, the work of a student is to learn more, whereas the work of a master is to hold the light or teach—to help others evolve. What level do you mainly operate in?

3D ~ Student
* Wonder about your spirit and consider what "lights your fire with joy"
* Stop seeking approval from others and accept your own Divinity

3D ~ Apprentice
* Focus on the things you love and appreciate about yourself; do so out loud
* Take time to notice the activities that bring you peace and engage in them
* Affirm that you are loved by your Creator

4D ~ Journeyperson
* Look into people's souls
* Recognize the Spirit within all beings

5D ~ Master
* Laugh at your ego and enjoy your Spirit
* Be open to your Divine Nature

Which level do you feel you mostly resonate in? _____

How can you connect more with your Divine Nature? _____

_____

_____

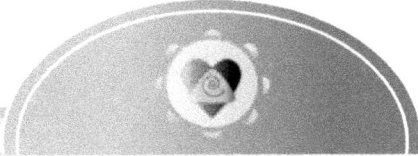

EXERCISE #62
Your Special Lesson's Life Purpose

"For each of us, as individual souls, however, there is, in any incarnation, a particular purpose for being here. We have special lessons to learn, and until we truly experience and understand our lessons, we continue spiraling through an endless cycle of experiences (and incarnations even), with these lessons presented to us in numerous different ways." (p. 69)

"The two primary archetypes of Love and Will manifest in our personalities in a variety of ways. Very simply, we can say that most people tend to be more developed in their connection to one of these archetypes and relatively under-developed in their connection to the other." (p. 70)

~ Will Parfitt, *The Elements of the Qabalah*

Our life purpose reflects our growth and expansion toward self-realization. The process balances the aspects of ourselves—Love and Will.

Will is the ability to be self-determined, directing and focusing your energy and attention in a desired direction. Too much Will can result in being manipulative, selfish, and ambitious. Too little creates fear of becoming powerless.

Love is the ability to be cooperative, sensitive, caring, and receptive, and to express unconditional love and acceptance. Too much love will create a sense of attachment, dependency, and conformity. Its underlying fear is of loneliness and being totally bereft of love.

Which one are you mainly focused on now?

_____

_____

_____

_____

_____

Exercise #63
Your Mastery of Life's Life Purpose

THE GAME OF LIFE

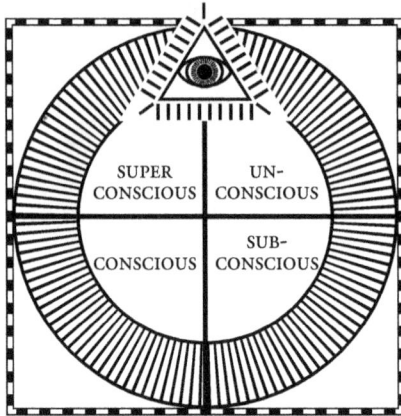

SUPER CONSCIOUS | UN-CONSCIOUS
CONSCIOUS | SUB-CONSCIOUS

"As the player moves deeper into the conscious quadrant, his ability to reason becomes sharper and sharper. Once again using the human body as an analogy, he realizes that an organ or system cannot know or understand its purpose or function by observing other organs or systems. It can only know its function by revelation, that is, watching without judgment to see how it functions. What would happen to the body if the heart made a determination about its purpose studying the lungs or intestines? The same principle applies to each player. Each purpose can only be revealed. It cannot be decided by looking at what another player is being, doing, or having." (p. 58)

"By the time a player reaches the final round of the conscious quadrant, he has enough self-awareness to know what his talents and abilities are. By age seven, in any given lifetime, he already knows what he is drawn to naturally." (p. 59)

~ Carolyne Fuqua, *Mastering the Game of Life*

Think back to when you were seven. What natural gifts and talents did you have an insatiable desire to share and express? _____

_____

_____

What were you naturally drawn to? _____

_____

_____

On the journey through the quadrants, what has been revealed to you about your purpose through dreams, visions, epiphanies, or divine communications?

_____

_____

_____

Your Spiritual Identity's Life Purpose

"What is meant by your 'spiritual ideal'? Is it something that is unconscious, something known only to your soul? Is it that sense of ideal and purpose that your soul intended upon incarnating? . . .

"What is the best conscious understanding that you currently have of this deep sense of ideal which is held by your soul for this lifetime? Or put more exactly, what label can you put on that sense of personal identity from which your purpose shall be lived? Who is this Self that [Edgar] Cayce calls your individuality? Have you caught a glimpse or two of yourself as this identity? Have you had special moments in which you knew yourself in a different way?" (p. 88)

~ Mark Thurston, *Discovering Your Soul's Purpose*

Create a mind map for yourself of all that you hold sacred or ideal by drawing, in the center a circle or heart, and drawing lines or spokes from that center where you identify those times when you were compelled in some unusual way to act from something that touched you deeply inside. Put that experience in the circle or heart.

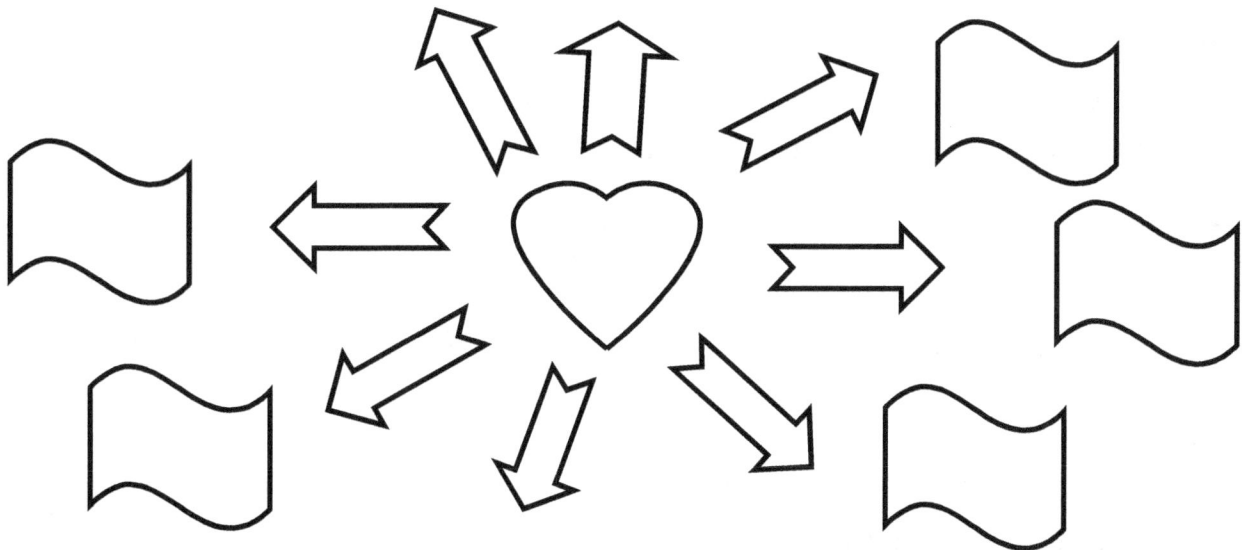

What things spark the passion or spiritual ideal that has been present in your life?

_____

_____

EXERCISE #65
Your Path's Life Purpose

"You have the ability to choose which path to walk:
The path of flesh or the path of Spirit." (p. 81)

~ Danna Demetre, *What Happened to My Life?*

The Path of the Flesh

What would it take for you to be or feel contented, satisfied, fulfilled, or complete in your skin? List all the earthly wants or goals that would give you that sense of fulfillment or contentment.

_____

_____

_____

_____

_____

The Path of Spirit

What guidance have you received on how to be or feel contented, satisfied, fulfilled, and complete? Write down all the guidance and its direction.

_____

_____

_____

_____

_____

What purpose is revealed to you through your Flesh and Spirit? What wants to be birthed or expressed through you? _____

_____

_____

Exercise #66
Your Metaphor's Life Purpose

"The word meta means that which 'stands between, comes after, or stands for.' A metaphor is an image that can create a bridge between different meanings, showing the likeness between them, or representing something else by transferring meaning from one object or event to another." (p. 155)

~ Joseph Chilton Pierce, *Evolution's End*

What image, vision, or dream keeps recurring in your life? _____

_____

_____

What do you stand for or have a commitment to? _____

_____

_____

What person do you admire and would want to emulate? Why?

_____

_____

_____

What do you perceive as that person's life purpose? _____

_____

_____

Is there some way to personally express that metaphor's life purpose? _____

_____

_____

_____

_____

EXERCISE #67
Your Intuition's Life Purpose

"Intuitive experiences include, but are by no means limited to, mystical insights into the nature of reality (purpose). Experiences which are commonly called intuitive also include discovery and invention in space, inspiration in art, creative problem solving, perception of patterns and possibilities, extra sensory perception, clairvoyance, telepathy, precognition, retrocognition, feelings of attractions and aversion, picking up 'vibes,' knowing or perceiving through the body rather than the rational mind, hunches and premonitions." (p. 57)

~ Frances Vaughan, *Awakening Intuition*

Spend some time with each of these techniques—perceiving patterns, ESP, clairvoyance, precognition, and picking up vibes—to see what naturally comes to you or has already come to you many times during your life.

What artistic visions have you had that give you a glimpse of your reality and possibility?

_____

What creative problems have you solved or do you have a natural aptitude to excel at?

_____

Can you see global patterns that have been affecting your life? _____

_____

Have ESP visions or "vibes" about what your purpose is been revealed to you?

_____

What would mastery look like in this area for your Self? _____

_____

Have any past lives revealed your purpose for this incarnation? _____

_____

What things do you feel the most natural doing or have an unexplained gift for?

_____

Your Incarnating Reason's Life Purpose

"Some people said they came back to help others, and to grow spiritually themselves. Some said they came to acquire new experience as a supplement to what they had already done in other lives, or to correct tendencies that were ingrained over several lifetimes. Some said they came to become more social after lifetimes of relative isolation and impoverishment. Others said they came to work out personal karmic relationships." (p. 44)

~ Carol Adrienne, *The Purpose of Your Life*

Which aspects of these Life Purposes do you have a connection or resonance with? Circle all that apply.

* Directing your living energy in ways that matter personally in order to be co-creative with your life force energy

* Following your inner guidance to people, places, and things so that life happens synchronistically for you.

* Learning to love yourself and others more fully, deeply, and unconditionally

* Focusing on a particular characteristic, such as faith, trust, courage, helping others, and so on

* Helping others in their path of spiritual development

* Finishing up karmic connections with a person, place, or thing

* Doing activities and things you have a passion for

* Creating moments of authenticity, transcendence, and spiritual awakening in your life

What has the strongest pull for you to accomplish? _____

_____

_____

_____

EXERCISE #69
Your Psyche's Life Purpose

"Some may be here to bring light into the world; others to retrieve infinite treasures of darkness. Some may celebrate the miracle of existence by inspiring us through song, others through dance, or through the visual arts, or science. Some may be here to give form to a certain range ideas, or cultural practices, or stories. Others are here to heal people, to understand, to nurture. The answer is waiting in the part of the human psyche that nature herself gave birth to: the human soul." (p. 308)

~ Bill Plotkin, *Soulcraft: Crossing into the Mysteries of Nature and the Psyche*

Your psyche has brought you many Soul images. Circle all that apply.

◆ You peek into your psyche and have non-ordinary experiences of images through daydreams, deep imagery, trance states, fasting, sexual ecstasy, illness, coma, or drug-induced states. What has been revealed to you?

◆ You notice expressions that speak from your soul, like a voice, dance, or science providing insight or direction.

◆ You feel powerful emotions such as hope, desire, gratitude, and joy. You feel "emotional depth" like nothing before, often followed by sadness.

◆ You have a desire to heal, nurture, or understand people and a desire to act on it. How would you like to express this? _____

In what way does your vision serve and benefit the whole community? _____

_____

How does this purpose or vision compel you to action? _____

_____

What have you experienced like this? _____

_____

What has it compelled you to do? _____

_____

Exercise #70
Your Divinely Guided Life Purpose

"Well, you made me understand when you said, 'We're not God, just part of God and that part of us is in Earth's school and learning. We're in God's school." (p. 178)

~ Diane Ladd, *Spiraling Through the School of Life*

What do you feel God is trying to have you learn or teach you? _____
_____

What Divine messages do you keep getting that you are not listening to but that keep coming? _____
_____
_____

What do you feel could be the purpose for these messages? What do you feel you are being taught in your life? _____
_____

How do your lessons purposefully lead to your life purpose, and what steps are you taking to learn more? _____
_____

What would mastery look like in this area for your Self? _____
_____
_____

What Divine direction is this teaching pointing you in? _____
_____

How do you feel you could most purposefully express that Divine direction in your daily life? _____
_____
_____

Your Purpose for Your Life's Life Purpose

"You are here on the planet for a reason. There is a purpose for your life. When you become clear about your mission, a deep feeling of inner contentment begins to develop within you. You truly know that every experience in your life is propelling you forward in alignment with your mission." (p. 67)

~ Denise Linn, *Soul Coaching*

Denise has an exercise to explore the purpose for your life by watching the signs, coincidences, and synchronicities. With each experience or feeling during the day, ask how the underlying message relates to your purpose.

What showed up in your world today? _____

_____

What were the messages telling you? _____

_____

Now complete the following statement over and over. Keep filling it in until you experience a sense of release, joy, and exaltation about your soul's mission.

The purpose of my life is _____

The purpose of my life is _____

The purpose of my life is _____

The purpose of my life is _____

The purpose of my life is _____

The purpose of my life is _____

The purpose of my life is _____

The purpose of my life is _____

The purpose of my life is _____

The purpose of my life is _____

EXERCISE #72

Your Spiritual Potential's Life Purpose

"Spiritual potential lies in one's horizontal and vertical actions. It is not just how much you affect others around you (horizontal). It is also how well you connect with and operate in multilevel communication and connection (vertical). Your spiritual potential relates to both 'directions.' Over the past two and one half years, you have trained and disciplined yourself to connect with and receive clear, usable information from various levels available to the soul. . . . You are experiencing being on the threshold of change. It is quite difficult to relax during these times because the 'threshold of change' means that one is still living out the old patterns but has vision into and is moving toward the new patterns." (pp. 154–155)

~ Machaelle Small Wright
Dancing in the Shadow of the Moon

What are the things that you do (or want to do) in the "horizontal" direction that make a difference and have an impact on the planet? _____

_____

_____

What divine communications or guidance (vertical connections) have you received? Write down what you have been guided to do. _____

_____

_____

How is it that you have been shown (vertical communication) or figured out how to integrate and implement (horizontal) aspects of your life together? _____

_____

_____

What do they tell you about your purpose? _____

_____

_____

_____

Exercise #73
Your Being in Life's Flow Life Purpose

"To explain this I have to say something about the way my mind works; the way I view and move through life. Simply put, I don't think. I don't make choices or decisions. I don't weigh possibilities and select one over the others. Instead, I observe patterns and move with them. I have a refined sense of rightness and not-rightness that guides me in all things. No decision in my life is made through ratiocination [a reasoned train of thought]. I wait for unfolding. I sense currents and I flow with them.

"You don't have to be enlightened to operate this way; you just have to release the tiller. Once you do, an entirely new way of flowing through life opens to you; a way that is based on rightness and sensitive to non-rightness. So when I look at my own life, my own story, I look for the pattern, the unifying theme, the sum of the parts that explains my existence." (p. 145)

~ Jed McKenna, *Spiritual Enlightenment*

Describe any feelings of "rightness" you have experienced that guide you. These expressions are aspects of your Life Purpose. _____

_____

Do you have any feelings of "non-rightness" about things you shouldn't be doing or things that rub you the wrong way? _____

_____

What do the "flow" patterns in your life point toward? _____

_____

Where does your flow (without the filter of your mind) want to take you? Where would you ideally like to go? _____

_____

What experiences of this "rightness" have you had before? _____

_____

_____

EXERCISE #74

Your Soul's Expression Life Purpose

"Taking a step toward soul life during the full light of the workday, we begin a journey toward a subterranean world that until now we have only explored after-hours, during the drive home, or in the silence of the small hours. Like any journey into neglected places, this journey has a natural drama to it. The cost of failure, as I point out in the stories and poetry that follow, is very high, but the prize is an experience of work that can benefit the spirit as much as the pocket, a nourishing approach to work that may make the moment equally as fulfilling as the years of patient sacrifice." (pp. 7–8)

~ David Whyte, The Heart Aroused

Allow yourself to go on a journey within, a journey of wondering and curiosity without censoring yourself. Let yourself go on a drive, daydream, or hike. Take a break during the day when you are so moved and look at the contrasts in your life. What things would you love to be doing if money and time were no object? Why do you want to be doing them? _____

_____

_____

What about those things would be fulfilling to you? What purpose do you want to express through them? _____

_____

_____

Notice any part(s) of yourself that feel dormant and would like to come out of the closet or let their hair down so you could just be yourself. What are you wanting to be, do, or have at the deepest level of your being? _____

_____

_____

_____

_____

Exercise #75

Your Spiritual Embrace's Life Purpose

"A most incredible awareness tool in the coaching process is establishing life purpose. It is our divining rod to stay aligned with Spirit. Once we know our purpose, we can more easily understand how Spirit guides us. During coaching experiences, Spirit constantly prods and pokes, saying, 'Listen, feel it, do it.' When a client embraces Spirit, an awareness of the next step or risk emerges; when action is taken, it feels right." (p. 201)

~ Teri-E Belf, *Coaching with Spirit*

Do the following visualization and see what Spirit is guiding you to do. Imagine yourself being taken to a place that brings you a great deal of joy, where you are totally engrossed in what you are doing and lost in the flow . . . Then let yourself focus clearly on what exactly you are doing. Notice the qualities of what it is as you feel deep inside yourself. What is being fed and given birth to? Let your Spirit guide you through this birth and blessing that you are being and doing.

Describe what you visualized or were guided to do or in some way sensed as your direction and purpose. _____

_____

_____

_____

What do you always seem nudged to do? _____

_____

_____

How does it relate to the guidance you received from the visualization?

_____

_____

_____

_____

Your Actor's Life Purpose

"Reincarnation means evolution, he [Lammers] explained: the evolution of the spirit of man through successive lifetimes on earth—sometimes as a man, sometimes as a woman, now as a pauper, now as a prince, here belonging to one race, there to another—until finally the spirit has reached perfection enjoined on us by Christ. The soul is like an actor who takes different roles and wears different costumes on different nights." (p. 32)

~ Gina Cerminara, *Many Mansions*

Imagine yourself as an actor. You can take the stage and play any part your heart desires. Let your imagination, creativity, and desire run free! Use your active imagination for this. Here are some possible thoughts to get you started:

If time, money, and fear were not issues, what would you be doing? _____

_____

Ponder these thoughts: I wonder what I would be doing if I were _____

_____

If I were a _____, I can see myself doing

_____

I have always seen myself as or doing _____

_____

I feel as though I have done _____ before—

it just comes so naturally to me.

What are the threads for you in these activities? _____

_____

_____

The part I most like playing is _____ because it makes

me feel _____ about myself.

Your Treasure Within's Life Purpose

"The Emerald Child is a treasure that lies deep within you, a sparkling jewel that radiates passion, vitality, and fearlessness. Representing boundless possibility and inexhaustible energy, this aspect of Self encourages you to reach for the stars, to settle for nothing less than everything that you imagine and desire . . . When we become adults, it is the persistence of our Emerald Child that allows us to be playful, to see the goodness in others, to meet each day with happy expectancy, and to look forward to the future." (p. 98)

- Renee Welfeld, Your Body's Wisdom:
A Body-Centered Approach to Transformation

Do this visualization for yourself:

Settle into a quiet place where you can imagine and reconnect with your Emerald Child. Watch him or her closely. Then ask your Emerald Child to share with you his or her passions and those things that he or she desires beyond anything else. Write down what is revealed to you. Then thank your Emerald Child for coming to visit you.

_____

_____

_____

_____

_____

_____

_____

_____

_____

_____

_____

Your Dimensional Life Purpose

"More and more people are awakening to the fact that we have choices to make and the possibility that realities beyond our third dimension really do exist. This awakening has appeared limited and has the nature of a grassroots movement, but it is truly part of a much bigger picture: the evolution of humanity back toward the light of creation." (p. 160)

~ Meg Blackburn Losey, *The Secret History of Consciousness: Ancient Keys to Our Future Survival*

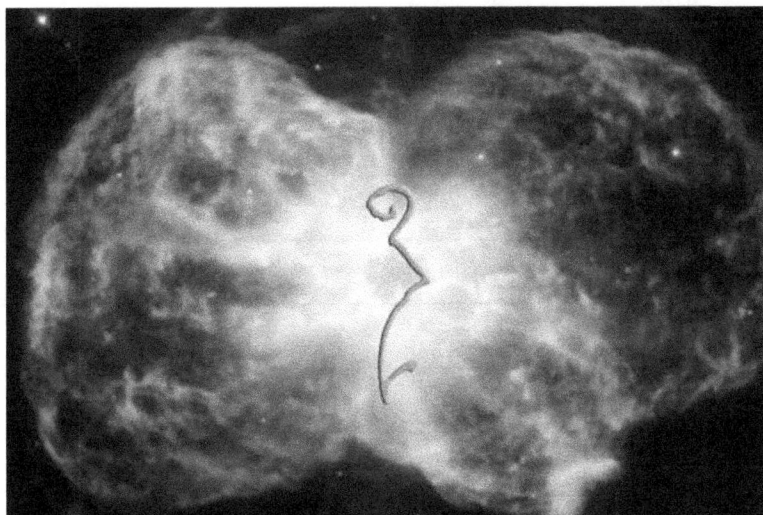

This image is adapted from Meg's "Meditation 8 ~ Courage Amid Change." Do this meditation and let it flow to see what arises from your consciousness. It will show you a facet of your purpose.

"Look deep within yourself. Can you find the innocence you felt as a child—that sense of wonderment when you encountered something new and exciting? As a child, you didn't hesitate to explore whatever piqued your curiosity. Instead, you leapt into discovering it. Imagine how you can bring that childlike curiosity into this now, bringing excitement for the changes to come and your imaginings about what magic those changes will bring you." (pp. 180–181) What showed up for you?

_____

_____

Exercise #79

Your Higher Self's Life Purpose

"Deep within her, a voice awakened, her soul's promise to give her life in service
to Prime Creator and the awakening of heaven on earth." (p. 139)

~ Judith K. Moore
Song of Freedom: My Journey from the Abyss

Spend 30 minutes listening to your own voice within—your Higher Self. What is it sharing with you? Write down your experience. _____

_____

_____

_____

What are you here to share? _____

_____

_____

_____

_____

What direction does it give you? _____

_____

_____

_____

What is the path for you to take? _____

_____

_____

_____

_____

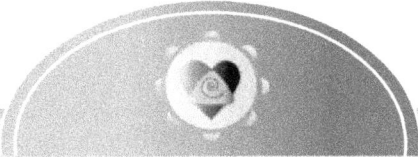

Exercise #80

Your Midlife's Life Purpose

"I feel that I've missed my calling in life. How do I find it?
I've successfully reached midlife. Is that all there is? What's next?
I've been growing spiritually. How do I connect my spiritual growth to my work?
I'm in a major transition (divorce, job loss, retirement, graduation,
death of a loved one, illness). How do I find meaning and direction?
I have enough material success. How do I find fulfillment?" (p. 2)

~ Richard J. Leider, *The Power of Purpose:*
Creating Meaning in your Life and Work

Ask your Future Self the answer to each of these questions by doing a guided meditation in which you imagine your ideal day. Life feels complete, and you have a sense of fulfillment in your life. Start the meditation with waking up in the morning. What time do you wake up? Where are you? What do you do with your morning and day? What satisfies and fulfills you about your day? You can also explore the questions in the quote and ask to be given the answers. (For people who are older, do a retrospective on the life you've lived. What is yet to be done?) _____

_____

_____

_____

_____

_____

What else was revealed to you about your life, purpose, and fulfillment?

_____

_____

_____

_____

_____

EXERCISE #81

Your Archetypal Themes' Life Purpose

"Each of us has all the great archetypal themes hidden inside. We all have the seeds
of the heroic quest with us; we must live it out sometime, on some level. Each of us
has the journey and labors of Psyche, the encounter with Eros and Aphrodite, built
somewhere into our inner structure. One can't avoid these archetypal leitmotivs;
one must express and experience them." (p. 153)

~ Robert Johnson, *Inner Work*

Sit with yourself in a place and with time to explore and use your own active imagination.
In active imagination, you focus your mind, heart, and soul on a mythic theme that,
if you were God in the universe, you would like to do or experience. Let yourself
actively imagine and explore the scenes and let the events play out fully with your
total involvement. Perhaps you want to be a warrior and make something right or a
feminine archetype who might want to be the nurturing mother to many. Let your
imagination and inner desires run free. What is revealed to you of this hidden yearning
or archetypal theme and purpose for being?

_____

_____

_____

_____

_____

_____

_____

_____

_____

_____

_____

Exercise #82
Your Creators' Life Purpose

"I hope that you never lose your sense of awe over all the gifts that the Creator has built into your being, whether the Creator is God or your own creative soul intent on experiencing the wonders of living here on this glorious planet in the wondrous vessel known as your body." (p. 303)

~ Debra Lynne Katz, *You Are Psychic*

Let your mind and imagination daydream, let your mind wander, or let your guidance shine through. What outcome have you come here to help create on the planet? What path is revealed for you to follow?

Step into your power as a Creator. What do you want to create on this planet?

_____

_____

_____

_____

What gift do you feel the Creator, God, or your Soul wants you to express here on earth? _____

_____

_____

Let your mind and imagination wander and let your guidance shine through. . . . What is the outcome you are here to manifest?

_____

_____

What is the path that is revealed for you to follow?

_____

_____

EXERCISE #83

Your Living Thing's Life Purpose

"Another method of mind expansion practiced by the Native Americans has been that of becoming, which is actually a mind stretching practice. While it is used in many ways, its primary purpose is to deepen one's relationship with the rest of creation . . . To do this you must become something else . . . a rock, a spider, a tree or another person. A faceted crystal will help you consider the various aspects of the subject at hand." (p. 286)

~ Thomas E. Mails
Secret Native American Pathways: A Guide to Inner Peace

Settle into a quiet place where you can visualize and connect with another living thing—whether animal, mineral, plant, or human. Feel yourself stepping into the energy of your focus so you can truly feel, sense, and connect to its energy and what is emanating from it. Sense what it has come here to do. What are you being shown?

_____

_____

_____

If you have trouble visualizing, use your active imagination to envision something and watch what happens. Get a sense of the purpose of the living thing and how it executes that purpose on the planet. Write down what is revealed to you. _____

_____

_____

What made you choose the particular thing you chose? _____

_____

_____

_____

_____

Your Ancestor's Vision Life Purpose

"You have a gift to give this world just by being you. And NO ONE ELSE can give that gift. You are the only you there is. If I could look deep into your eyes, I know I would travel through the tunnel of light and see the signature of your soul that is unique and beloved to Spirit. I see in the realm around you, beings who have compassion for you, ancestors who want to bring guidance, animals and angels who are supporting you. You are not alone. I can see that. I salute you. I would wish for you to find the meaning of your life as well as the comfort and courage which are needed as part of each day." (p. 60)

~ Sharon Blessum, *Luminous Journeys*

Reflect on your life. Light a candle in the darkness and invite your ancestors, deceased loved ones, and beloved animals who are no longer with you to join you. Ask them to guide you. Let them take you on a journey to understand the meaning and purpose of this lifetime—what in particular you came here to do. Be quiet, explore with an open heart, and be present to the Great Mystery. Let it answer your questions and your heart's desire. What did it reveal or show you? _____

_____

_____

_____

Who was there with you and for you? _____

_____

How do you experience your purpose differently now? _____

_____

_____

_____

_____

Exercise #85
Your Gifts' and Lessons' Life Purpose

Purpose

"All happens for a reason, perfection is everywhere, have faith in divine order,
less confusion will be there. Every meeting is a sacred one, a dual 'gift' exchange,
each offers a new awareness, where the minds engage.

There are two main perceptions, 'gifts' or 'lessons' shown,
acceptance or resistance, is how each is known. No occurrences are by chance,
all messages have a role, offering increased awareness,
for assisting every goal." (p. 31)

~ Eric M. Brodsky
Poetry of the Angels: Inspiration for Us All

Sit quietly and play some beautiful angelic or New Age music that can take you into a meditative state. As in a ritual or prayer, ask your angels to guide you to your gifts and lessons that are part of the beautiful purpose you came here to accomplish. Another approach, before going to bed, is to ask your angels to show you in your dreams—let them en-lighten you!

Describe what they showed you and how you can see that being a facet or direction of your Life Purpose.

_____

_____

_____

_____

_____

_____

_____

_____

_____

Your Guides' Vision Reveals Your Life Purpose

"May God bless you, and your angels protect you. May your runners connect you, your helpers assist you, your healers support you, your teachers enlighten you, your joy guides delight you, your nature spirits balance you, your animal guides recall your soul, and your Higher Self lead you to live a life of peace, grace, creativity, and contribution filled with love and laughter on your personal earthly journey." (p. 254)

~ Sonia Choquette, *Ask Your Guides*

Do a series of silent or guided meditations in which you ask and connect with each group of guides listed below in whatever way is natural to you. Ask them what they know of your purpose for incarnating in this lifetime. Have them show you in a way that you can understand and receive their wisdom. What did each group tell you?

- Your Angels: _____
- Your Runners: _____
- Your Helpers: _____
- Your Healers: _____
- Your Teachers: _____
- Your Joy Guides: _____
- Your Nature Spirits: _____
- Your Animal Guides: _____

What is their consistent guidance about your purpose?

_____

_____

_____

_____

_____

EXERCISE #87
Your Soul's Cycle Life Purpose

"Changes in your plan can be taken more gracefully when you are aware of the Soul's plan. Develop new ways to look at the total picture to determine its purpose. Your level of maturity and your actions reflect the handling of change. Steps taken in acceptance and peace far outweigh steps taken in resentment and fear. Those who realize the purpose of their soul's plan progress farther to higher levels. The highly developed soul uses every situation as a learning experience and accepts it as part of the soul's cycle." (p. 84)

~ Sally Sharp, *Angel Prayers*

What do you feel is your Soul's plan? _____

_____

_____

How have the angels whispered to you about your purpose? _____

_____

_____

How have your dreams revealed to you at a soul level about your purpose? _____

_____

_____

Do fears or resentments keep coming up for you to resolve? Have you been given guidance on how to handle them but have refused to do it? _____

_____

_____

What is the purpose of events that keep happening to you? _____

_____

What is the next level of your Soul's growth represented by these events? _____

_____

Exercise #88

Your Sacred Visions' Life Purpose

"The 405 [Stone Men] powers are divided into four groups, each which renders service in a given area . . . A third group helps with dreams. These spirits use medicines to make a person dream, and then help the dreamer understand what the dream means. The last works with in the area of the inner person. They help the holy man and the medicine man look within himself and other creatures to see there the things that cannot otherwise be seen with the naked eye . . . This fourth division of spirits is also employed when, for example, a person comes to me and wants to know something about his innermost self. He wants to understand himself so that he can find peace and live in a more secure way." (pp. 50–51)

Thomas E. Mails, *Fools Crow*

Try this process to gain insight: Mails suggests going to a sacred place, a quiet place, where you can be uninterrupted for a long period of time. Ask the "405 Stone Men" or your guides to sit in a sacred circle, perhaps around a fire, and to give you guidance regarding your Life Purpose. Ask them to show you in your dreams or a vision what your purpose is and how you are supposed to express it. Write down your vision or dream. _____

_____

_____

_____

_____

What is it that you have been shown is your Life Purpose? _____

_____

_____

How is it that you've been guided to express that purpose? _____

_____

_____

Exercise #89

Your Visions' Life Purpose

"Our more gentle conversations with ourselves about things we love to be, do and have allow us to identify what we love in an investigatory, mental excursion, without ever doing anything about it. We venture into our imaginations, through memory, emotions, the senses, into the potentiality of growth." (p. 55)

~ George W. Meek
After We Die, What Then?

Whether or not you believe in reincarnation, what areas of growth—physical, emotional, mental, or spiritual—do you keep being called to or have déjà vu experiences about?

_____

_____

_____

Do you have any areas that you feel drawn to or, like a déjà vu, that you want to experience in this lifetime or repetitive experiences that keep happening again and again? Why do you think they keep happening? _____

_____

_____

_____

What do you feel is the purpose for these experiences that causes them to happen over and over again? _____

_____

_____

_____

_____

_____

_____

EXERCISE #90

Your Reincarnation's Life Purpose

"The principles of reincarnation, however, allow us to view life with a much broader perspective—from the standpoint of eternity. From this point of view, one brief lifetime is seen not as the beginning of our existence, but as nothing more than a flash in time, and we can understand that an apparently pious person who may be suffering greatly is reaping the effects of impious activities performed in this or previous lives. With this broader vision of universal justice we can see how each individual soul is alone responsible for its own karma." (p. 104)

~ Teachings of His Divine Grace A. C. Bhaktivedanta Swami Prabhupada
Coming Back: The Science of Reincarnation

What things do you feel subconsciously compelled to do, without any rational reason for doing them? _____

_____

_____

Is there anything or anyone that you are fixated on? If so, look at the reason for that and what purpose it could serve for your evolution or for the resolution of some karma.

_____

_____

_____

If you are experiencing any suffering, is there a part of you that wants this direct experience? Might you have purposefully asked for this experience (such as a quality, an emotional state, or disease)? If so, what might the reason be?

_____

_____

_____

_____

_____

Exercise #91
Your Pre-Earth Life Purpose

"Apparently the main purposes of pre-earth life experiences are for personal development and preparation for earth life. Among our pre-earth life activities are volunteering to come to earth, making covenants with spirits to come to earth as family and friends, selecting our missions and positions for life on the earth, preparing for the test and experiences of life on earth. In the pre-earth life, we associated with many people for eternities." (p. 46)

~ Craig Lundahl & Harold Widdison
The Eternal Journey

If you've ever had a near-death experience or past-life experience, you will have a sense of your life purpose or "mission" for this lifetime. If not, use a past-life regression audio from www.YouTube.com that you feel comfortable with to guide you to that place. These questions will help you clarify your purpose.

* What have you volunteered to come to Earth to do? _____

_____

_____

* What deep commitments or covenants have you made to people in your life? To whom and for what reason? _____

_____

_____

* Have you personally had a near-death experience and seen glimmers of your purpose or the reason you "died but came back"? What was revealed to you? _____

_____

_____

* What is your purpose for this incarnation? _____

_____

_____

Exercise #92
Your Past Lives' Life Purpose

"It is not out of keeping here to consider the Oriental belief that the soul is allowed one 'comfortable' reincarnation for every six lives of arduous development." (p. 93)

"He cited that Leonardo da Vinci as an example of a genius whose soul was expressing itself, now in the present, as it had never been allowed to do in his lifetime. The genius of da Vinci could only be expressed when the world had progressed sufficiently to recognize it and put his creations into practice." (p. 88)

~ Noel Langley
Edgar Cayce on Reincarnation

Find a YouTube guided visualization on past-life regression such as http://youtube.com /watch?v=BV6RHDHjYJA. Let it take you back through some of your past lives. What genius are you working to perfect or manifest here? Can you see or feel how you've been working on this for numerous lifetimes? _____

_____

What is being revealed to you about your journey through your past lives? _____

_____

_____

What have you been working on for many lifetimes that you are manifesting now? How does that reflect a purpose for your life? _____

_____

_____

What are the recurring themes you see or have experienced throughout these lifetimes?

_____

_____

_____

_____

_____

Your Spiritual Path's Life Purpose

"The first law is called the Law of the One. It is a law whose sole purpose is to assist each soul in its personal process of self growth." (p. 160)

"The Law of the One is simply a concept of interconnecting reality and the oneness of life. Each person will have a specific spiritual path that is co-determined by the spiritual guides (guardian angels and angelic judges) assigned to them and also by the Time Lords acting under the divine plan of the Supreme Creative Force (God). Everyone's goal is to discover and utilize their chosen spiritual path for personal growth and for service. This energy path is the Kha or the soul force itself." (p. 162)

~ Virginia Essene and Sheldon Nidle
You Are Becoming a Galactic Human

What is the chosen spiritual path you want to pursue by looking back at your past lives? _____

_____

What thread of lifetimes are you working with? _____

_____

_____

What did you come to further understand and evolve in this lifetime?

_____

_____

Do a past-life regression with a past-life regression professional or a hypnotherapist, or by using this guided meditation: http://www.youtube.com/watch?v=aWdJ6Tje-QE or one of your choice. Write down what the lifetimes revealed to you and what you have come here to do. _____

_____

_____

_____

Your Dreaming Life Purpose

"He [Jung] believed certainty of interpretation could be achieved only by analyzing a series of dreams over an extended period of time, perhaps years. Only in this way could he see fundamental ideas and themes of the dreamer's struggle, kaleidoscopically revealed through different aspects of the same situation." (p. 20)

~ Jill Morris, The Dream Workbook

Use a dream journal for at least one week. Ask before going to bed, or during daylight times when you can daydream, for your Life Purpose to be revealed to you in a way that you can understand upon waking. Then answer the following questions in your journal about each dream.

1. What do you feeling upon waking? _____

_____

2. What real-life memories or other dreams does this dream remind you of?

_____

3. What the setting of the dream—familiar or not? In nature, inside, or both?

_____

4. Did any colors in your dream jump out at you? What do they signify to you?

_____

5. Did anything from the previous day impact or influence this dream? _____

_____

6. What symbols, keywords, or phrases were strong in your mind when you awoke?

_____

7. What was the purpose for each of the actions of the characters in the dream?

_____

8. How did this dream convey your purpose to you? _____

_____

EXERCISE #95
Your Special Talents' Life Purpose

"Everyone has a purpose in life . . . a unique gift or special talent to give to others. And when we blend this unique talent with service to others, we experience the ecstasy and exultation of our own spirit, which is the ultimate goal of all goals." (p. 93)

~ Deepak Chopra
The Seven Spiritual Laws of Success

The seventh law is, "The Law of 'Dharma' or Purpose in Life." Chopra recommends that you keep a journal for two weeks and ask yourself, "What special gift do I naturally give to others?" and "How would I best like to use this in service to others?" Ask these questions of yourself after every meditation and write down all the answers that come to you. After that time, you will have a clearer idea of the types of activities that are aligned with your life purpose.

I have discovered that the activities I do naturally and love doing are (list them all):

_____

_____

_____

_____

_____

_____

_____

_____

_____

_____

_____

_____

Your Spiritual Qualities' Life Purpose

Day One (from 15-day journal)

"You come into this world attempting to fulfill certain qualities with yourself, and you go about it in many ways. But everyone has a prime directive: You are here to find out who you are, to find where your home in spirit is, to go there in consciousness, and to have co-creative consciousness with God, the Supreme Father. This is our whole direction and purpose on the planet. This is where your satisfaction and fulfillment lie." (p. 138)

~ John-Roger, *Spiritual Warrior:*
The Art of Spiritual Living

Read this quote to yourself several times a day and ask to have more revealed to you throughout your day or night. Then upon waking or before bed, read it again and journal about what comes up for you or answer the questions below.

1. What qualities do you want to express and fulfill in yourself?

   _____

   _____

2. What are the ways in which you'd like to express them?

   _____

   _____

3. Where is your Home? How are you supposed to create Home in a co-creative way that serves others in the process? _____

   _____

   _____

4. What do you want to do or say in the world? _____

   _____

   _____

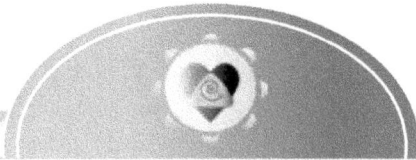

Exercise #97

Your Dreamwork's Life Purpose

"Dreams were seen as devices of the gods to communicate helpful and heuristic information to man . . . The first method was to envisage the content of the dream as a whole and then try to find some other context for the meaning of what was being said. . . . The second method was by use of a 'cipher,' that is, by treating the dream as if every image was a separate sign. For this a dream book was consulted." (pp. 48–50)

~ Montague Ullman, *Working with Dreams*

Before going to bed, ask your Higher Self to give you a dream or dream image that is a reflection of your Life Purpose and how you are to express it in your waking life. Just relax into sleep with no expectations of an outcome. In the morning, fill in this Dream Sheet.

Write out your dream in as much detail as you can remember. (Method One: your whole dream) _____

_____

_____

_____

_____

What feelings and insights came to you about your purpose from this dream?

_____

_____

_____

List specific images from the dream that stand out or have a lot of energy for you. Look up what they mean. (Method Two: look up the individual symbols from an online dream interpretation site) and learn what message they have for you.

_____

_____

Your Spirit's Vision Life Purpose

"There is an intimate impulsion to know your purpose for being on the planet and to live it. We are not simply talking about your profession here but about your overarching purpose for having a human incarnation ... With utmost sincerity ask within, 'What's Spirit's highest vision for my life?' When you ask such a question, you touch the heart of the Infinite, and when your intuition is attuned, you will receive a response. That response will have to do with generosity of spirit: it will have to do with the fact that your profession is only one of the vehicles through which you express your purpose and deliver your unique qualities of heart and spirit on the planet as only you can." (pp. 216–217)

~ Michael Bernard Beckwith
Spiritual Liberation

Sit quietly and ask your Spirit and Divine guidance to give you insight that you can make sense of in response to the question, "What is the highest vision for my life?" Patiently await the response. If you do this before going to bed, ask it to be revealed in a dream image, symbol, or sequence. What unique vision is revealed to you that makes your heart flutter, sing, or feel passion and a sense of being enlivened? Write down any images, thoughts, feelings, and directions that you were given.

_____

_____

_____

_____

_____

_____

_____

_____

_____

SECTION 7
Your Mystical Purpose

Your Energy & Beingness

* *Body-Based Exercises*
* *Sound-Based Exercises*
* *Joy, Bliss, & Enchantment Exercises*
* *Nature Exercises*
* *The Alpha & Omega*

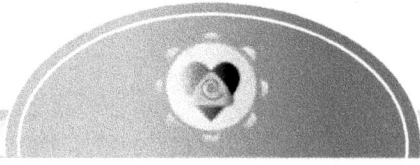

Your Energy & Beingness

This section is designed for people who have reached the self-realization or self-actualization and transcendence stages of Maslow's Hierarchy of Needs. It is in these stages that you are no longer "searching for your purpose." Rather, Being becomes your purpose—meaning living as energy and in the flow. You experience life from a place of vibrational awareness—a field in which you experience all the frequencies of Nature and the Divine. An example from antiquity is the Aboriginal Australians, who live in the "Dreamtime," which is the flow of energy and consciousness that is always present and alive for us to experience. This state of being is totally aware and conscious. It no longer uses 3D logic as a basis for functioning, and it follows its own rhythms for purposeful action while living in the flow.

The exercises in this section are designed to give you the experience of what it feels like to consciously be in the flow and live on purpose. The first exercises are body-based (meaning what you experience in your body) to open up the ability to feel the natural flow of energy, life, and purpose as it moves through you. The next set of exercises bring in sound, inviting it to wash through you—again presencing the vibratory field you can embody. The last exercises take you into a meditative state in which there is no self, to an experience of joy, bliss, awe, and enchantment, which have their own vibrations. I have added an exercise in nature which, if you are a nature lover, you can do several times. The final two exercises invite you to explore what you plan to do with your new insights and purpose moving forward.

I invite you to just be present with yourself and see what arises while doing this series of exercises. The 5D is not rational or logical—it is an expression, experience, vibration, embodiment, and field that we can tap into at any moment, where our purpose is only to BE . . .

Enjoy.

EXERCISE #99

Your Chakras' Life Purpose

"The seven sacred truths transcend cultural boundaries, and at the symbolic level they constitute a road map for our life journey—a road map imprinted in our biological design. Again and again the sacred texts tell us that our life's purpose is to understand and develop the power of our spirit, power that is vital to our mental and physical well-being." (p. 67)

~ Caroline Myss, *Anatomy of the Spirit: The Seven Stages of Power and Healing*

Do a meditation focusing your awareness on your energy centers. Feel into them and let your awareness experience each chakra. This meditation gives you a snapshot of the energy flowing in your body. The symbolism is from Caroline Myss. Write down what shows up for you in each chakra.

Name	Location & Lesson	Images, Sensations, & Feelings	What It Wants From You (Its Purpose)
First Chakra	Base of spine Material world		
Second Chakra	Below navel Physical desire, sex		
Third Chakra	At diaphragm Ego, self-esteem		
Fourth Chakra	Breastbone Love, compassion		
Fifth Chakra	Throat Self-expression, will		
Sixth Chakra	Third eye Mind, intuition		
Seventh Chakra	Top of head Divinity, spirituality		

Exercise #100

Your Toltec Creator's Life Purpose

"Toltec knowledge arises from the same essential unity of truth as all the sacred esoteric traditions found around the world. Though it is not a religion, it honors all the spiritual masters who have taught on earth. While it does embrace spirit, it is most accurately described as a way of life, distinguished by the ready accessibility of happiness and love." (p. xiv)

~ Don Miguel Ruiz, *The Four Agreements*

This exercise is designed for you to experience your autonomic breath—the rhythmic, automatic breathing that happens without your needing to do anything but relax. Be your breath flowing through you. This is a prayer and meditation from Don Miguel Ruiz to connect with our Creator and the happiness and love that are possible to experience (p. 132).

"Focus your attention on your lungs, as if only your lungs exist. Feel the pleasure when your lungs expand to fulfill the biggest need of the human body—to breathe.

"Take a deep breath and feel the air as it fills your lungs. Feel how the air is nothing but love. Notice the connection between the air and the lungs, a connection of love. Expand your lungs with air until your body has the need to expel the air. And then exhale, and feel the pleasure again. When we fulfill any need of the human body, it gives us pleasure. To breathe gives us much pleasure. Just to breathe is enough for us to always be happy, to enjoy life. Just to be alive is enough. Feel the pleasure to be alive, the pleasure of the feeling of love . . ."

Spend some time in this place of happiness and bliss. This is an expression of your Divine Self and purpose. What fills you with joy about this meditation? _____

_____

_____

_____

_____

_____

Your Musical Journey's Life Purpose

"Many people find that playing music can help them access that profound place. In this particular journey, I felt the wisdom surfacing even more so with every note from that charming instrument. By playing it, it opened doors of creativity for me—expanding myself in ways that I never thought were possible. It also seemed to me after experiencing this particular journey, more abundance and good fortune flowed into my life. Perhaps it was because of my strong focus and desire to move forward." (p. 106)

~ Rosanna Ienco, *Awakening the Divine Soul*

Follow these steps to connect with a higher power:

1. Play some favorite music that you use to relax or meditate, or you can explore different musical options on www.pandora.com.

2. Get into a comfortable, relaxed position, either sitting or lying down. Start with the intention to connect with a highly evolved part of yourself. Then close your eyes, take some deep breaths, and allow your breath to rhythmically travel through your body. Flow with the music moving you, follow your breath with the curiosity of your awareness, and see what arises. Ask for an experience of the magnificence of your being. Continue to take deep breaths and be open to whatever your Being is showing you.

3. Write down any images, thoughts, feelings, and directions you were given.

   _____

   _____

   _____

4. What sense does this give you of "who you are"? This is an energetic manifestation of your purpose. _____

   _____

   _____

   _____

Your Chanting Life Purpose

"Reflect on this. We forget our good days and we remember our bad days. This is why we feel nothing works—because our way of thinking is not always right. In the beginning, the practice of contemplation is soul-searching. You go through one tunnel after the other, you go through one pain after the other, one joy after the other. And sometimes, this reflection can become unbearable because you see yourself. Your whole life is presented before your eyes. Nevertheless, this reflection, this act of contemplation removes all that which is unnecessary. You're left lighthearted with only one thing: the experience of grace, the experience of Shakti, divine energy." (p. 51)

~ Swami Muktananda, *Meditate*

Do this meditation while chanting "Om Namah Shivaya," which is found in many videos on www.YouTube.com. As you meditate, let the music vibrate through you in order to experience inner happiness and inner peace. From that place, notice whatever visions arise about your Beingness or your sense of your authentic Self.

_____

_____

_____

_____

_____

_____

_____

Feel into your focus, direction, or purpose for being. What energetically comes through for you? _____

_____

_____

EXERCISE #103

Your Inner Knowing's Life Purpose

"Once we go through a true process of self-discovery,
No one can take away our self-confidence;
The inspiration comes from with in,
And we know without needing to be told." (p. 84)

~ Tarthang Tulku, *Gesture of Balance*

According to Tulku, "When we look at our ordinary experience with an attitude of openness, free from judgments or divisive concepts, we see 'subject' and 'object' naturally as one. In this way, the spiritual path becomes part of our lives—not just an abstract ideal reserved for special occasions. When meditative experience is truly part of us, spiritual qualities naturally express themselves in our daily lives, and we can be confident that our meditative awareness will carry us through whatever situations we encounter." (pp. 84–85)

Let yourself quietly enter a meditative state of well-being and experience the flow of your own divine connection with the Oneness. What arises from this stillness as the direction and flow for your energy?

_____

_____

_____

_____

_____

_____

_____

_____

_____

Note: This exercise can be repeated many times to experience your unique flow in the ever-changing present.

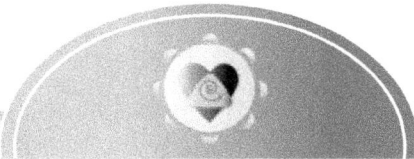

EXERCISE #104

Your Inner & Outer Life Purpose

"Your life has an inner and outer purpose.
The inner purpose concerns Being and its primary purpose is to awaken.
The outer purpose is secondary and your Doing." (p. 258)

~ Eckhart Tolle, *A New Earth*

What is it that your Being or Soul has a resonance with? _____

_____

_____

_____

When you are totally quiet in a meditative space, what does that Beingness want?

_____

_____

_____

_____

How can you execute this in your 3D life now? _____

_____

_____

_____

Are there things that you want to be doing differently from this place of insight—
ways you want to reorganize your life to more closely align with your Beingness?

_____

_____

_____

_____

Your Revelation's Life Purpose

"Recognition implies revelation. The ways in which our evolutionary potential—or 'God's presence at work in us,' as Father Thomas Keating says—is revealed through us in ways that are concrete, specific, and well known. The fruits and gifts of the spirit, the virtues as described by all faiths, such as charity, peace, kindness, joy, generosity, faithfulness, and gentleness, are concrete and specific revelations of aspects of our true nature in particular situations. We can immediately recognize and appreciate them when they appear because some innate faculty in us knows the good when we see it. That intelligence is lodged where our innate goodness resides: in our hearts." (p. 166)

~ Joan Borysenko & Gordon Dveirin
Your Soul's Compass: What Is Spiritual Guidance?

Sit quietly and spend some time with your Self as you focus on your heartbeat. Think of things that make you well up with tears or feel deeply moved and touched. Let yourself feel the "gifts of the spirit" mentioned above. Which ones most shine through you?

_____

_____

What are some of the ways you have expressed these gifts or witnessed these gifts being expressed by others that profoundly impacted you? _____

_____

_____

How do you use these divine, God-given gifts on a regular basis in your life?

_____

_____

Is there an underlying purpose or intent in your actions? _____

_____

_____

_____

Your Numinous Life Purpose

"Glimpsing a world that transcends our mental universe of data and logic may produce within us a powerful longing to live in that transcendent state. Living with the numinous that surrounds us is like fulfilling the mystic's longing to come close to the eternal presence felt in moments of visionary ecstasy. Too often we place mystical experience outside the range of the ordinary person, and yet we can each have our moments of awe and enchantment." (p. 301)

~ Thomas Moore
The Re-Enchantment of Everyday Life

Create a list of the ways that you experience awe or enchantment in your daily life. (It can be in any area of your life.) _____

_____

_____

In what ways do you experience the numinous, or what Moore defines as "the seizure by the beautiful, experience of the immense, or catastrophic"? Another way to word it might be: What takes your breath away and takes you to a different reality?

_____

_____

How does this consistently show up in your life? _____

_____

_____

What purpose does it have in your life? _____

_____

_____

What do you do that gives you the greatest satisfaction, whether or not it's for money? _____

_____

EXERCISE #107
Your Ecstatic Life Purpose

"In a broader sense, shamanism is the aboriginal heritage of all of us. Whenever the sources of the universe reach down into the embodiment of the human image in corporeal bodies, the shaman emerges as a source of ecstatic regenerative powers. Shamanic experience is present in the lives of those of us in the modern world who are searching for the whole, the eternal, the ecstatically true embrace of reality amid the fragmented, chaotic, and false remnants of lost traditions." (p. 17)

~ Rowena Pattee
Compiled and Edited by Gary Doore
Shaman's Path: Healing, Personal Growth and Empowerment

List five situations that bring you the most joy or create ecstatic moments in your life where you are totally immersed in your experience.

1. _____
2. _____
3. _____
4. _____
5. _____

What do they have in common? For instance, all in Nature, relating to a child, having an invigorating experience, something miraculous happening, or a peak experience.

_____

_____

_____

How can you create more ecstatic experiences for yourself? _____

_____

What happens to you as a result of those experiences? How do you want to incorporate those experiences once you "return to this reality"? _____

_____

Your Bliss-Filled Life Purpose

"Meditate on your Self.
Honor your Self.
Worship your Self.
Understand your own Self." (p. xi)

"The Upanishads suggest that the entire universe is created out of the bliss of
God, that it arises from bliss, lives in bliss, and in the end merges in bliss. So this
bliss, which comes from God, is our birthright." (p. 1)

~ Swami Muktananda
Kundalini: The Secret of Life

Create an awareness or meditative state for yourself in which you can be relaxed, calm,
and free to experience your bliss—the joy that flushes spontaneously through you. Feel
it and just enjoy the experience. Then debrief by writing your answers below.

How do you define bliss and joy for your Self? _____

_____

What qualities and aspects of your Self bring you the most joy? _____

_____

Meditate on your Self: What would or does bring you bliss? _____

_____

When you truly honor your Self, what is there that brings your Being great joy?

_____

When you imagine your Self as an aspect of God, what brings you absolute joy and
bliss about your Beingness? _____

_____

If you were to worship your Self for the Being that you are, how would you celebrate
your Self? What are you most proud of that you feel deserves to be celebrated?

_____

Exercise #109

Your "Who I AM" Life Purpose

He Said "I AM"

"What if Jesus did not instantly know who he was? Or what his gifts were? What if it dawned on him only gradually, as it dawns on each of us? Maybe his mother recited stories of the unusual events surrounding his birth. Maybe she set the beautiful boxes the three wise men brought him on a shelf in his room, and at night the young boy would take them down and hold them and wonder. Or perhaps he knew instantly that he had a special calling and was just awaiting the moment when his powers could be set free. Either way, I believe Jesus had to go into the wilderness to find out who he was—that a wilderness experience was as much a part of his shaping and destiny as it is of yours and mine." (pp. 3–4)

~ Laurie Beth Jones, *Jesus CEO*

Go out into the wilderness or nature to a place of reverence where you feel at home. Be still there and lose yourself in the environment. Let things quietly arise within you. Let your experience unfold. When you return from the wilderness, describe your wilderness experience—when you were lost and not sure where to turn or where to go. What did you learn about yourself and who you are? _____

_____

_____

_____

What gifts could you see more clearly or feel in yourself? _____

_____

_____

_____

Write or draw three positive and powerful images about yourself. Examples: I am a rainbow or I am an eagle. _____

_____

_____

EXERCISE #110

Your Alpha & Omega Life Purpose

"As you journey to this point which is the sum total of who you are, knowing all these things, you arrive at a moment when it is time to share your knowledge with your family, society and culture. Many of you are poised in this moment. You have a duty to share what you know—not to preach or sow seeds of fear or plant the field for another, but to vibrate in the wholeness of who you are. You need to understand and encompass all the things that make up society—life, death, birth, children, and all society's members, young and old, not simply those whom you consider to be productive. Radical change will occur. Have compassion as you put the things you have learned to work." (p. 243)

~ Barbara Marciniak
Earth: Pleiadian Keys to the Living Library

As you contemplate the completion of these exercises and your journey, how is what you've learned going to benefit you? These important elements of your life can have an impact on your Life Purpose. Write down what arises in your experience for each group.

- Your Family: _____

- Your Friends: _____

- Society: _____

- Culture: _____

- Your Religious/Spiritual Practice: _____

- Your Work: _____

- Your Career: _____

_____

_____

_____

_____

_____

EXERCISE #111

Your Soul's Life Purpose

"When we make even a meager attempt to live in the present, our Souls provide us access to the wisdom of Spirit, and everything séems to make perfect sense, even the bad things. No longer standing on flat terrain and suffering from limited vision, we are lifted to the summit of the mountain and can see forever. We understand that there is no reason to fear because we now know, beyond a shadow of a doubt, that we are Spirit, and the Spirit is eternal." (p. 44)

~ Tami Coyne, *Your Life's Work: A Guide to Creating a Spiritual and Successful Work Life*

Create your "Spiritual Resume"—a resume that reflects your Soul's work and what you have accomplished that is personally meaningful to you. (See Section 9, pages 178–180 for examples.)

Here are some questions to stimulate your thought process:

1. What is your connection to God or the Creator?

2. Why is your life meaningful?

3. What brings you joy?

4. What are your definitions of happiness and fulfillment?

5. What dreams or aspirations have you accomplished?

6. What do you consider as your God-given or Divine gifts and talents?

7. How have you used these gifts or talents to make the world a better place?

8. What is your spiritual mission or objective for this lifetime?

9. Imagine your ideal Soul-filled profession and career. What is it?

_____

_____

_____

_____

Know Your Purpose

Discovery of Your Life Purpose

- *Your Life Purpose Answer Sheet*
- *Your Life Purpose Synthesis Sheet*
- *Your Top 10 Life Purpose Themes*
- *Blank Life Purpose Answer Sheet*
- *Suzanne's Life Purpose Synthesis Exam*

Your Life Purpose Answer Sheet

Synthesize the answers of the exercises you have completed in the workbook and write them down on this page.

Step 1: Hone down your twenty-five completed answers from the exercises into specific themes in order to get a clear direction of your purpose. (See page 170 for an example of the author's worksheets.)

1. _____
2. _____
3. _____
4. _____
5. _____
6. _____
7. _____
8. _____
9. _____
10. _____
11. _____
12. _____
13. _____
14. _____
15. _____
16. _____
17. _____
18. _____
19. _____
20. _____
21. _____
22. _____
23. _____
24. _____
25. _____

My overall understanding of my purpose is: _____
_____
_____

Your Life Purpose Synthesis Sheet

Take your answers from the previous page and focus them into the specific themes for a clear sense of your direction and purpose.

My **Developmental Purpose** (from p. 30) is _____ and I am expressing it by _____ .

My **Natal Purpose** (Sec. 2, pp. 31–38) revealed to me that

1. _____
2. _____
3. _____

My **Psychological Purpose** (Sec. 3, pp. 39–62) suggests that I prefer

1. _____
2. _____
3. _____

My **Professional Purpose** (Sec. 4, pp. 63–80) is to express skills, gifts, and talents by

1. _____
2. _____
3. _____

My **Transitional Purpose** (Sec. 5, pp. 81–102) is to refocus my efforts toward

1. _____
2. _____
3. _____

My **Spiritual Purpose** (Sec. 6, pp. 103–146) guides me to

1. _____
2. _____
3. _____

My **Mystical Purpose** (Sec. 7, pp. 147–162) flows in the direction of

1. _____
2. _____
3. _____

My **overall understanding of my purpose is:**

1. _____
2. _____
3. _____

Your Top 10 Life Purpose Themes

Step 2: Write down your "Top 10 Recurring Life Purpose Themes" from Step 1. These should be phrases that keep appearing as you synthesize your life purpose into specific themes and a clear direction.

1. _____
2. _____
3. _____
4. _____
5. _____
6. _____
7. _____
8. _____
9. _____
10. _____

Step 3: Write down your "Life Purpose Statement" that encompasses all the ideas, energy, passion, and vision in your "Top 10 Recurring Life Purpose Concepts" from above. You may rewrite this sentence several times until it has the clarity, feeling, and Truth of being your Life Purpose. This statement may be very lofty and more conceptual because it will encompass so much of who you are. You will see reflected in your statement the goals, values, and ideals that you value most.

_____
_____
_____
_____
_____
_____

Step 4: Do a retrospective of your previous jobs, careers, and endeavors and see how each one of them has in some way been a manifestation of your Life Purpose or gave you tools to help you manifest your Life Purpose. Celebrate and honor your journey!

_____

_____

_____

_____

_____

_____

_____

_____

Step 5: Explore how and in what ways you would like to accomplish your Life Purpose in the present and going forward into the future that would be the most fulfilling and would express your true potential.

_____

_____

_____

_____

_____

_____

_____

_____

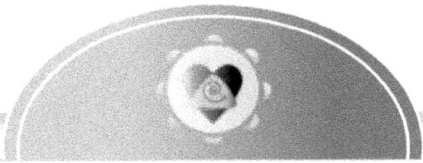

Blank Life Purpose Answer Sheet (EXTRA SHEET)

If you want to delve into something more deeply than you have room for on the pages provided, feel free to copy this sheet and insert as needed.

1. _____
2. _____
3. _____
4. _____
5. _____
6. _____
7. _____
8. _____
9. _____
10. _____
11. _____
12. _____
13. _____
14. _____
15. _____
16. _____
17. _____
18. _____
19. _____
20. _____
21. _____
22. _____
23. _____
24. _____
25. _____
26. _____
27. _____
28. _____
29. _____
30. _____
31. _____

Suzanne's Life Purpose Synthesis & Example

Step 1: Here are my exercises and what they revealed to me as an example of how I have synthesized these answers into my own life purpose.

Section 1—Your Developmental Purpose

⬧ I am a Boomer in the Self-Actualization phase of my life.

⬧ I always want to know more about the unseen world and how reality and Universal Truths work.

⬧ I envision my life as being a self-employed coach who creates, manages, and directs my own life.

⬧ My focus is on balancing all aspects of life—3/4/5D—and helping people find that balance for themselves.

Section 2—Your Natal Purpose

⬧ *Astrology*—My sun sign is Scorpio, and I love the spiritual side of life. I am a water sign, so I understand and want to use both the emotional and the intuitive to connect with the unseen world of Spirit and to help others make that type of connection for themselves.

⬧ *My name's meaning*—Suzanne means "white lily" and "peace." I create peace and harmony by resolving or bringing together the dualities in life.

Section 3—Your Psychological Purpose

⬧ *My Personality Type*—I am an INFJ, and I use my type to sense into things intuitively to get my bearings before taking action. I need to be alone and have time to explore the unseen realities to get my answers.

⬧ *My Awakened Will* wants to figure out ways to connect the unseen world with this reality in ways to share that with other people.

⬧ *My Spiritual Ministries are:*
Discernment—to know and listen to divine messages
Encouragement—the ability to guide and help others
Passion—about sharing the message
Faith—I trust God and am helped to overcome obstacles.
Knowledge—I share the wisdom that God reveals to me with others.

⬧ *My Energetic Purpose*—I am open moment by moment to the guidance and direction that I am given by God/Spirit to know how to proceed in my days' activities.

⬧ *Frankl's Meaning* for me of work is trying to do something significant by contributing to the spiritual growth and development of the planet.

Section 5—Your Transitional Purpose

◆ *My Making a Life Life's Purpose*—The investments I use going forward in making my life are spiritual—my connections with the Divine, my spiritual life experiences, and being able to share them in meaningful and productive ways, such as screenplays/movies and ebooks or other informational products.

◆ *My Fulfilled Dreams*—I want to be recognized for my creativity as a "transformational life coach or alchemical artist" through my films, books, and vision as well as the various ways I present these concepts to make a difference. I want to be a new thought leader and a recognized life purpose expert.

◆ *My Altruistic Life*—I would like to create a foundation to help at-risk kids have the opportunity to meet their own Future Self to see how their lives can turn out and to give them practical and spiritual tools to accomplish this. It makes me happy when I've made a difference in someone's life!

◆ *My Growing Edge Life Purpose*—I want to step out into bigger spheres of influence with my 3/4/5D work and create a large following for my ideas.

◆ *My Legacy's Life Purpose*—The Spirit, Nature, and You Foundation, which helps people on their divine path and through their times of existential crisis

Section 6—Your Spiritual Purpose

◆ *My Spiritual Ideal* is fun and full of life, spontaneity, love, joy, exuberance, connections with other people, and sharing, like a big game of Twister only of the spirit. I am called by Spirit to spontaneously act without thinking.

◆ *My Chakras* want to give voice to my spiritual ideas and ideals.

◆ *My Special Talent* is to be able to convey unseen or spiritual experiences and energy in ways that people can have a direct experience of for themselves.

◆ *My Creator*—Archangel Uriel wants me to express how we are all divinely connected and to give people the opportunity to experience that magnificence, grandeur, and perfection of our spiritual beings and this world as we are.

◆ *My Tarot Card* is "The World." I am always in the quest and exploration of something bigger than I know and bringing it "down to earth."

Step 2: Take your answers from the previous answer sheets and begin to synthesize them into specific themes for your clear direction and purpose. Use brainstorming to write down the things that keep repeating until you get to the kernel or core—the "Top 10 Elements of Your Life Purpose."

1. Self-Actualization

2. The Unseen World

3. Universal Truths

4. Doing it on my own, in my own time, and in my own way

5. Expressing my creativity

6. Writing, screenplays, coaching, and speaking

7. Bringing downloads of energy and ideas into being to share with others

8. Being a public figure and thought leader

9. Using my voice—both written and spoken—to make visible to people the unseen world and higher dimensional consciousness

10. Being an energetic channel for whatever knowledge wants to come through

Step 3: As you write down the words or phrases in Step 2, let your mind begin to synthesize them into the one thought that encompasses them all. This is an organic process and may take a few attempts. Write it proudly – this is your Life Purpose!

Here's mine . . .

MY LIFE PURPOSE is to connect humanity with the Divine in practical ways so that their conscious vibration will fulfill them and enrich the planet!

Suzanne Strisower
November 11, 2011

Step 4: Now it's time to do a retrospective of your life. Review all the exercises you have completed as they relate to your life. Look at how everything you have done in your life is related to accomplishing your life purpose. Honor yourself and how diligent you have been on your journey. Recognize that you have instinctively been trying to accomplish your life purpose from the beginning.

Step 5: Look forward. Write your life purpose resume with your 3/4/5D skills, incorporating your new insights. How do you feel that you most passionately, effectively, and intuitively want to express your purpose? Make whatever changes to your life you feel are needed in order to be aligned with your life purpose and who you are presently.

Blessings to each of you for your commitment and desire
to be a conscious and contributing member of humanity
and to know what you came here to do this lifetime.

Suzanne Strisower, MA, PCC ~ Your Next Step Coach

Note: If, in the future, your life changes and you feel lost, you can go back and review or repeat this process using whichever exercises you feel drawn to in order to hone your purpose for that phase of your life.

SECTION 9
Resources

Templates, Websites, & Bibliography

- *Mind Mapping Template*
- *Resume Templates*
- *Online Resources*
- *Bibliography*
- *About Suzanne*

Life Purpose Mind Map Template

Creating a "Mind Map" or brainstorming means letting concepts flow as they naturally do. You can do this in an organized way as an outline, shown below, or in a more organic way. Search online for mind-mapping techniques that resonate with you. A great site is www.xmind.com, which offers simple and free ways to create a mind map for yourself. Mind maps start with a topic or main idea (shown in caps), followed by all the different subtopics (marked with an asterisk) that are part of the main topic, followed by the ways you execute each one (shown as the indented items), followed by what actually is done (shown on the right of each colon).

My Life Purpose is "TO SHARE MY KNOWING & BEING" by . . .

* **TEACHING:**
  Live Classes: POD mtgs. ~ Creating a Great Life™
  Teleseminars: You are RIPE for Change™
  Informational Products
  Workshops

* **CREATING THINGS:**
  Screenplays: SHILEAH Trilogy ~ High Times Growing ~ Foster Kids
  Books: 111 Inspirational Life Purpose Quotes . . . ~ Revised Rune Book
  Articles: Life Purpose ~ Stages of Life ~ Fulfillment ~ You Have a Multidimensional Life
          Purpose ~ Healing Your Emotional Being
  Oracles: Online Readings ~ Personal Rune Oracles for People

* **HEALING:** Reiki ~ Energy work ~ Recalibration & Reclamation work
  Negative Emotions into Positive Energy ~ Using 3/4/5D

* **LOVING LIFE IN ITS MANY EXPRESSIONS:**
  Nature ~ My animals ~ My "Kyuds" dogs, my menagerie of llamas, sheep, goats, chickens
  My gardens ~ My many fruit and nut trees
  My Platinum Ray POD ~ Learning and connecting with the Beings of Light ~ Dreaming and
  the Dreamtime ~ Connecting with kindred spirits/like-minded people ~ Being with Great
  Spirit/Archangel Uriel ~ Meeting my many guides and being mentored by them ~ Connecting
  with the Earth

* **QUALITIES OF MY LIFE PURPOSE**
  Passion and curiosity about things ~ Connection with the Divine/Angels of Light ~
  Guidance of Great Spirit/Archangel Uriel ~ Dreaming into life ~ Being in the question ~
  Knowing the Universal Truth ~ Love of life ~ Understanding 3/4/5D ~ Being with nature

Life Purpose Resume Example

Now you are going to take all of the qualities that you have discovered about your Life Purpose and put them into a "resume format." Include all the things that you love in each of the categories. Here's mine . . .

Suzanne Strisower, MA, PCC

PO Box 559, Oroville, CA 95965-0559 Phone: (530) 589-5889 Email: Suzanne@YourNextStepCoach.com
Website: www.YourNextStepCoach.com   Rune Website: www.InsightfulRunes.com

Life Purpose Objective: To use my guidance to work co-creatively with Spirit and to create products and services that empower, inspire, and help humanity move into the higher vibration of the New Age

3D ~ Professional Experience and Work History
• Being a Lifestyle Entrepreneur and creating viable business models that are based on my optimal life purpose expressions
• Energetic, highly creative, inner-directed individual who has created radio shows, written screenplays, and authored many articles and books
• Loves people and wants to empower and inspire them in their interactions and undertakings
• Has numerous skills to connect and communicate with others—an excellent written and verbal communicator as well as reader of people's body language
• Curious and always wanting to optimize every aspect of life, both personally and professionally
• Respected lecturer, teacher, and workshop leader with unique, well-researched topics
• Use hypnotherapy, readings, and intuitive gifts to help others open up to their spiritual side
• Clearly articulate 3/4/5D life force energies and patterns to optimize each dimension

4D ~ Guidance and Inner Knowing
• Follow my guidance and know how to listen to Spirit through its many forms of expression
• Comfortable with many different disciplines, traditions, and aspects of spirit
• Listen to guidance to do intuitive and psychic readings for others to help them connect to their life purpose and flow
• Co-creating my right livelihood with Spirit, not bound by traditional jobs or thought processes, know how to translate spiritual guidance into practical action

5D ~ Energetic Connection to Self & the Cosmos
• Feel the cosmic energies flowing in and through me, receive downloads from Source

CLASSES & WORKSHOPS
Creating a Great Life Class™ ~ 8-week course and online course
Being a Lightworker ~ Living Your Purpose™ ~ 2-hour workshop/teleseminar
Successfully Reinvent Yourself for Professionals in Transition™ ~ 2-hour workshop/teleseminar
You are R.I.P.E. for Change™ ~ 4-week teleseminar series
Find Your Purpose in Life™ ~ Teleseminar and workshops

FEATURE FILM SCREENPLAYS & BOOKS
SHILEAH, a spiritual feature film screenplay, second screenplay of a trilogy
The Runes of the Four Realms; 111 Inspirational Life Purpose Quotes and Exercises to Find Your Life Purpose; a "Life Purpose Tweet" book, co-author of best-selling book *Be Happy, Healthy and Wealthy: A Guidebook for Women* and the upcoming book from Wake Up Women Be You: *Spread Your Wings and Fly*

Lifestyle Entrepreneur in Resume Format

Rewrite your resume so it reflects your Life Purpose as your objective and summary of qualifications. This resume is structured like a traditional resume. Here's the resume format that I have used to get a 50 percent response rate from potential employers.

Suzanne Strisower, MA, PCC
PO Box 559, Oroville, CA 95965-0559 Phone: (530) 589-5889 Email: Suzanne@YourNextStepCoach.com
Website: www.YourNextStepCoach.com   Rune Website: www.InsightfulRunes.com

Objective: To work in environments and with people whom I can help to expand their consciousness and use their life purpose and spiritual side in their workplace to create a triple bottom line for the employer.

Professional Spiritual Experience and Work History
2006–Present	Spiritual Life Purpose and Career Coach, Your Next Step Coach and Awaken to Your Life Purpose Coach
2010–Present	Radio Show Host, Living Well Talk Radio, weekly conscious living talk radio shows including: Living Life on Purpose, The DR's INN, Between Our Sheets with the Doctors, Your Life and Purpose Revealed, Between Our Sheets with Authors, and Wake Up Women LIVE!
2000–Present	Author and Publisher, *The Runes of the Four Realms*™, a New Age rune oracle, *111 Inspirational Life Purpose Quotes and Exercises to Find Your Purpose in Life*, and a "Life Purpose Tweet" book
1995–1998	Professional Weekly Intuitive, Claremont Hotel & Spa, Berkeley, CA
1990–Present	Intuitive and Workshop Presenter and Lecturer

Education and Specialized Training
M.A., Counseling Psychology, Pacifica Graduate Institute, Santa Barbara, CA
B.F.A., Interior Design, John F. Kennedy University, Orinda, CA
Professional Certified Coach (PCC), International Coach Federation, Lexington, KY
Certified Life Purpose and Career Coach, Life Purpose Institute, San Diego, CA
Certified Life Coach, Coach for Life, San Diego, CA

PRESENTATIONS/SPEAKING ENGAGEMENTS and PUBLICATIONS
Find Your Purpose in Life™ ~ 2-hour workshop, Butte College, CA
Living Well Talk Radio™ created and hosted weekly conscious living radio show on 96.7FM
Coaching an Inspired Profession, *Lotus Guide*, May/June 2007
What Are Runes? ~ Interview, KHSL TV Channel 12, Chico, CA
The Power of the Runes ~ 30-minute television segment for "Adventures in Health"
Hypnosis and the Biblical World ~ Guest lecturer, University of Miami, Miami, FL
Understanding and the Release of Stress ~ Continuing Education for Nurses, Concord, CA
Your Inner World Connection with Nature ~ California Department of Forestry Convention, CA
Creating a Great Life Class™ ~ 8-week course, Oroville Center for Spiritual Living
You Are R.I.P.E. for Change™ ~ 4-week teleseminar series
Spiritual Awareness and Practice in Everyday Life,™ ~ Ongoing classes working with Spirit

AWARDS & RECOGNITIONS
1993 Who's Who of American Women

Online Resources

NOTE: Search the author if a listed website is no longer live.

1. ASSESSMENTS

There are many free online assessments. Just use that as your search term for whatever type you are looking for.

2. PROFESSIONAL & CAREER RESOURCES

- Occupational Information Network (O-NET) - publishes the Occupational Outlook Handbook - http://www.online.onetcenter.org

3. PRACTICAL & PSYCHOLOGICAL RESOURCES

- Danna Demetre - http://dannademetre.com/
- Donna Dunning - Personality Typing - http://www.dunning.ca/
- Kimberly Fulcher - http://www.kimberlyfulcher.com/
- Bernard Haldane - http://www.dependablestrengths.org
- James Hollis - http://www.jameshollis.net/books/default.htm
- Kathleen Hurley & Theodore Dobson - http://www.9types.com/dave/index.html
- Robert Johnson - http://innerworkjohnson.blogspot.com/2007/06/dream-3.html
- Laurie Beth Jones - http://www.lauriebethjones.com/
- Robert Kiyosaki - https://www.richdadcoaching.com/
- Caroline Myss - http://www.myss.com/library/contracts/three_archs.asp
- Parker J. Palmer - http://www.couragerenewal.org/parker
- Steve Pavlina - http://www.stevepavlina.com
- Carol Pearson - http://www.herowithin.com/system.htm
- Bill Plotkin - http://www.animas.org/newbook/aboutBill.htm
- William A. Sadler - http://www.thirdagecenter.com/books.htm
- Barbara Sher - http://www.barbarasher.com
- Murray Stein - http://www.murraystein.com/articles.html
- Andrew Weil - http://www.drweil.com
- Susan K. Whitbourne - http://www.happiness-after-midlife.com/susan-whitbourne.html
- David Whyte - http://www.davidwhyte.com

4. TRANSITIONS ~ RESOURCES

- Gene Cohen - http://changingminds.org/books/book_reviews/
- Michael Farrell - http://www.midlife-men.com/
- Marc Freedman - http://www.encore.org/staff

5. SPIRITUAL RESOURCES

- A. H. Almaas - http://www.ridhwan.org
- Jose Arguelles - http://www.lawoftime.org/
- Martha Beck - http://marthabeck.com/index11.php
- Michael Bernard Beckwith - http://www.agapelive.com/
- Joan Borysenko - http://www.joanborysenko.com/
- Kevin & Kay Marie Brennfleck - http://www.liveyourcalling.com/liveyourcalling/author
- Deepak Chopra - http://www.chopra.com/
- Sonia Choquette - http://www.TrustYourVibes.com
- Christian Career Center - http://www.ChristianCareerCenter.com, see career exploration section
- Danna Demetre - http://dannademetre.com/women_of_purpose (Christian)
- Virginia Essene - http://www.sharefoundationnetwork.com/vessene.htm
- Susanne Fincher - Mandalas - http://www.creatingmandalas.com/
- Carolyne Fuqua - http://circlesoflight.net/
- Jerry and Esther Hicks - http://www.abraham-hicks.com/lawofattractionsource/index.php
- Rosanna Ienco - http://wolvesdenhealing.com/index.php option=com_content&task=view&id= 76&Itemid=133
- Debra Lynne Katz - http://debrakatz.com/Debra_Lynne_Katz.html
- Robert Kiyosaki - http://www.richdad.com
- Craig Lundahl - http://www.near-death.com/experiences/research19.html
- Jed McKenna - http://www.spiritualteachers.org/jed_mckenna.htm
- Judith K. Moore - http://www.recordsofcreation.com
- Jill Morris - http://www.wellsphere.com/brain-health-article/dream-symbols-18-types-of-dreams-part-2-lucid-dreams-and-the-senoi/684881
- James Redfield - http://www.celestinevision.com
- John-Roger - http://www.john-roger.org
- Dane Rudhyar - http://www.khaldea.com - astrology site
- Don Miguel Ruiz - http://www.miguelruiz.com
- Jamie Sams - http://www.jamiesams.org/core.html

- Robert Schienfeld - http://www.bustingloose.com
- Marsha Sinetar - http://www.marshasinetar.com
- Mark Thurston - http://www.paraview.com/thurston/index/htm
- Eckhart Tolle—http://www.eckharttolle.com
- Tarthung Tulku - http://www.zhaxizhuoma.net
- Montague Ullman - http://www.siivola.org/monte/papers_grouped/index.htm
- Frances Vaughan - http://www.francesvaughan.com/identity_maturity_and_freedom_ transpersonal_and_existential_perspectives_103994.htm
- Pastor Rick Warren - http://www.PurposeDrivenLife.com
- Owen Waters - http://www.InfiniteBeing.com
- Machaelle Small Wright - http://www.perelandra-ltd.com

Bibliography

1. Adrienne, Carol. *The Purpose of Your Life: Finding Your Place in the World Using Synchronicity, Intuition and Uncommon Sense.* New York: William Morrow, 1998.

2. Almaas, A. H. *Diamond Heart: Book One: Elements of the Real in Man.* Berkeley, CA: Diamond Books, 1987.

3. Arguelles, José A. *Earth Ascending: An Illustrated Treatise on the Laws Governing Whole Systems.* Boulder, CO: Shambhala, 1984.

4. Beck, Martha. *Steering by Starlight: The Science and Magic of Finding Your Destiny.* New York: Rodale, 1988.

5. Beckwith, Michael Bernard. *Spiritual Liberation: Fulfilling Your Soul's Potential.* New York: Atria Books (Simon and Schuster), 2008.

6. Belf, Teri-E. *Coaching with Spirit: Allowing Success to Emerge.* San Francisco: Jossey-Bass/Pfeiffer, 2002.

7. Blessum, Sharon. *Luminous Journeys: Natural Portal to the Spirit World.* Bloomington, IN: Xlibris Corporation, 2001.

8. Borysenko, Joan. *Your Soul's Compass: What Is Spiritual Guidance?* Carlsbad, CA: Hay House, 2007.

9. Brennfleck, Kevin and Kay Marie. *Live Your Calling: A Practical Guide to Finding and Fulfilling Your Mission in Life.* San Francisco: Jossey-Bass Publishing, 2004.

10. Brodsky, Eric M. *Poetry of the Angels: Inspiration for Us All.* Broomfield: Universal One Publishers, 1999.

11. Brolus, Tim. *Baby Boomers Almanac: How to Attain, Secure and Enjoy Your 3 Most Important Assets.* Macomb Township. MI: Better Living Publishing, 2006.

12. Cerminara, Gina. *Many Mansions.* New York: William Morrow & Co., 1950.

13. Chopra, Deepak. *The Seven Spiritual Laws of Success.* San Rafael, CA: Amber-Allen Publishing, 1994.

14. Choquette, Sonia. *Soul Lessons and Soul Purpose: A Channeled Guide to Why You Are Here.* Carlsbad, CA: Hay House, Inc., 2007.

15. ————. *Ask Your Guides: Connecting to Your Divine Support System.* Carlsbad, CA: Hay House, Inc., 2006.

16. Cohen, Gene D. *The Creative Age: Awakening Human Potential in the Second Half of Life.* New York: William Morrow & Co., 2000.

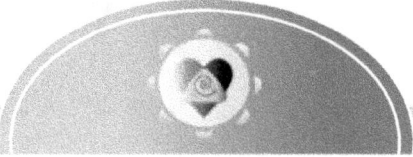

17. Coyne, Tami. *Your Life's Work: A Guide to Creating a Spiritual and Successful Work Life.* New York: Berkeley, CA, 1998.

18. de Chardin, Teilhard. *The Phenomenon of Man.* New York: Harper & Row, 1959.

19. Demetre, Danna. *What Happened to My Life?* Grand Rapids, MI: Revell, 2010.

20. Doore, Gary. *Shaman's Path: Healing, Growth and Personal Empowerment.* Boston: Shambhala, 1988.

21. Dunning, Donna. *What's Your Type of Career? Unlock the Secrets of Your Personality to Find Your Perfect Career Path.* Palo Alto, CA: Davies-Black Publishing, 2001.

22. Erikson, Erik H. *The Life Cycle Completed: A Review.* New York: W. W. Norton & Company, 1983.

23. Essene, Virginia E. and Nidle, Sheldon. *You Are Becoming a Galactic Human.* Santa Clara, CA: S.E.E. Publishing Company, 1994.

24. Farrell, Michael F. and Rosenberg, Stanley D. *Men at Midlife.* Dover, DE: Auburn House Publishing Co., 1981.

25. Fincher, Susanne F. *The Mandala Workbook: A Creative Guide for Self-Exploration, Balance, and Well-Being.* Boston: Shambhala, 2009.

26. Frankl, Viktor E. *Man's Search for Meaning.* Boston: Beacon Press, 2006.

27. Freedman, Marc. *Encore: Finding Work that Matters in the Second Half of Life.* New York: Public Affairs, 2007.

28. Fulcher, Kimberly. *Remodel Your Reality: Seven Steps to Rebalance Your Life and Reclaim Your Passion.* San Jose: RiverRock Press, 2006.

29. Fuqua, Carolyne. *Mastering the Game of Life.* Beverly Hills, CA: Circles of Light Publishing, 1996.

30. Gerzon, Mark. *Listening to Midlife: Turning Your Crisis into a Quest.* Boston: Shambhala, 1992.

31. ———. *Coming Into Our Own: Understanding the Adult Metamorphosis.* New York: Delacorte Press, 1992.

32. Goodman, Linda. *Star Signs.* New York: St. Martin's Press, 1987.

33. Haldane, Bernard. *How to Make a Habit of Success.* New York: Warner Books, 1975.

34. Hicks, Esther and Jerry. *Ask and It Is Given: Learning to Manifest Your Desires.* Carlsbad, CA: Hay House, 2005.

35. Hill, Robert D. *Positive Aging: A Guide for Mental Health Professionals and Consumers.* New York: W.W. Norton & Company, 2006.

36. Hodgson, Joan. *Reincarnation through the Zodiac.* Vancouver: CRCS Publications, 1979.

37. Hollis, James. *The Middle Passage: From Misery to Meaning.* Toronto: Inner City Books, 1993.

38. Hurley, Kathleen V. and Dobson, Theodore E. *What's My Type?* New York: HarperOne, 1992.

39. Ienco, Rosanna. *Awakening the Divine Soul.* Winchester, UK: John Hunt Publishing Ltd, 2009.

40. Johnson, Richard P. *The New Retirement: Discovering Your Dream.* St. Louis, MO: World Press, 2001. Self-published PDF, http://www.icoachidesign.com/info/retirement-book-intro.pdf

41. Johnson, Robert A. *Inner Work: Using Dreams and Active Imagination for Personal Growth.* San Francisco: HarperCollins, 1986.

42. Jones, Laura Beth. *Jesus, CEO: Using Ancient Wisdom for Visionary Leadership.* New York: Hyperion, 1995.

43. Katz, Debra Lynne. *You Are Psychic.* Woodbury, MN: Llewellyn Publications, 2004.

44. Kloser, Christine. *The Freedom Formula: How to Put Soul in Your Business and Money in Your Bank.* Dallastown, PA: Love Your Life, 2008.

45. Kiyosaki, Robert. *Teach to Be Rich: Awaken Your Financial Genius.* Rich Press, 2006.

46. Ladd, Diane. *Spiraling Through the School of Life.* Carlsbad, CA: Hay House, 1996, 2006.

47. Langley, Noel. *Edgar Cayce on Reincarnation.* New York: Paperback Library Inc., 1967.

48. Lansky, Bruce. *10,000 Baby Names.* Deephaven, MN: Meadowbrook, Inc., 1985.

49. Leider, Richard J. *The Power of Purpose: Creating Meaning in Your Life and Work.* San Francisco: Berrett-Koehler Publishers, 1997.

50. ————. *Something to Live For: Finding Your Way in the Second Half of Life.* San Francisco: Berrett-Koehler Publishers, 2008.

51. Levinson, Daniel J. *The Seasons of a Woman's Life.* New York: Ballantine Books, 1996.

52. Linn, Denise. *Soul Coaching.* Carlsbad, CA: Hay House, 2003.

53. Losey, Meg Blackburn. *The Secret History of Consciousness: Ancient Keys to Future Survival.* San Francisco: Weiser Books, 2010.

54. Lundahl, Craig A. and Widdison, Harold A. *The Eternal Journey: How Near-Death Experiences Illuminate Our Earthly Lives.* New York: Warner Books, 1997.

55. Mails, Thomas E. *Secret Native American Pathways: A Guide to Inner Peace.* Tulsa: Council Oak Books, 1988.

56. ————. *Fools Crow.* Lincoln, NE: University of Nebraska Press, 1979.

57. Marciniak, Barbara. *Earth: Pleiadian Keys to the Living Library.* Rochester, VT: Bear & Co, 1994.

58. McKenna, Jed. *Spiritual Enlightenment: The Damnedest Thing.* N.p.: Wisefool Press: 2009. www.WiseFoolPress.com

59. Meek, George W. *After We Die, What Then?* Columbus: Ariel Press, 1987. Metascience, 1980.

60. Mills, David. *10,000 Days: A Call to Arms for the Baby Boom Generation.* Lexington: Create Space, 2008.

61. Moore, Judith K. *Songs of Freedom: My Journey From the Abyss.* Flagstaff, AZ: Light Technology Publications, 2003.

62. Moore, Thomas. *The Re-Enchantment of Everyday Life.* New York: Harper Collins, 1996.

63. Morris, Jill. *The Dream Workbook.* New York: Little Brown & Co. Fawcett Crest, 1985.

64. Muktananda, Swami. *Kundalini: The Secret of Life.* South Fallsburg, NY: SYDA Foundation, 1979.

65. ————. *Meditate.* Albany: State University of New York Press, 1980.

66. Muller, Wayne. *How Then, Shall We Live? Four Simple Questions That Reveal the Beauty and Meaning of Our Lives.* New York: Bantam Books, 1996.

67. Myss, Caroline. *Anatomy of the Spirit: The Seven Stages of Power and Healing.* New York: Three Rivers Press, 1996.

68. Palmer, Parker J. *Let Your Life Speak: Listening for the Voice of Vocation.* San Francisco: Jossey-Bass, 1999.

69. Parfitt, Will. *The Elements of the Qabalah.* New York: Barnes & Noble Books, 1991.

70. Pavlina, Steve. www.StevePavlina.com

71. Pearson, Carol S. *The Hero Within.* San Francisco: Harper-Row, 1986.

72. Peterson, John. *A Vision for 2012: Planning for Extraordinary Change.* Golden, CO: Fulcrum Publishing, 2008.

73. Pierce, Joseph Chilton. *Evolution's End: Claiming the Potential of Our Intelligence.* San Francisco: Harper Collins, 1992.

74. Plotkin, Bill. *Soulcraft: Crossing into the Mysteries of Nature and the Psyche.* Novato, CA: New World Library, 2003.

75. Potter, Beverly A. *Finding a Path with a Heart: How to Go from Burnout to Bliss.* Berkeley, CA: Ronin Publishing, 1994.

76. Prabhupada, A.C. Bhaktivedanta Swami. *Coming Back: The Science of Reincarnation.* Los Angeles: The Bhaktivedanta Book Trust, 1985.

77. Ray, Paul and Sherry Anderson. *The Cultural Creatives: How 50 Million People Are Changing the World.* New York: Harmony Books, 2000.

78. Redfield, James and Adrienne, Carol. *The Celestine Prophecy: An Experiential Guide.* New York: Warner Books, 1995.

79. Roger D.S.S., John, with Kaye D.S.S., Paul. *Serving & Giving: Gateways to Higher Consciousness.* Los Angeles: Mandeville Press, 2009.

80. ————. *Spiritual Warrior: The Art of Spiritual Living.* Los Angeles: Mandeville Press, 1997.

80. Ross-Krieger, Erica. *Seven Sacred Attitudes: How to Live in the Richness of the Moment.* Reno: Still Mountain Press, 2005.

81. Rudhyar, Dane. *The Pulse of Life: New Dynamics in Astrology.* Distributed by St. Paul, MN: Llewellyn Publications, 1963.

82. Ruiz, Don Miguel. *The Four Agreements.* San Rafael, CA: Amber-Allen Publishing, 1997.

83. Sadler, William A. *The Third Age: 6 Principles for Growth and Renewal after Forty.* Jackson, TN: De Capo Press/Perseus Publishing Group, 1999.

84. Sams, Jamie and Carson David. *Medicine Cards.* Santa Fe, NM: Bear & Company, 1988.

85. Schachterle, Susan. *The Bitch, The Crone and The Harlot: Reclaiming the Magical Feminine in Midlife.* Santa Rosa: Elite Books, 2007.

86. Scheinfeld, Robert. *The 11th Element: The Key to Unlocking Your Master Blueprint for Wealth and Success.* Hoboken: Wiley and Sons, 2003.

87. Sharp, Sally. *Angel Prayers.* Minneapolis: Trust Publishing, 1994.

88. Sher, Barbara. *Live the Life You Love: In Ten Easy Step-by-Step Lessons.* New York: Delacorte or Random House Publishing, 1996.

89. Sinetar, Marsha. *Do What You Love, The Money Will Follow: Discovering Your Right Livelihood.* New York: Dell Publishing, 1989.

90. Stein, Murray. *Transformation: Emergence of the Self.* College Station: Texas A&M University Press, 1998.

91. Streep, Peg (Editor). *An Awakening Spirit: Meditations by Women for Women.* New York: Viking/Penguin, 1993.

92. Thurston, Mark. *Discovering Your Soul's Purpose.* Virginia Beach, VA: A.R.E. Press, 1984.

93. Tolle, Eckhart. *A New Earth.* New York: Dutton/Penguin Plume Book, 2005.

94. Tulku, Tarthung. *Gesture of Balance.* Berkeley, CA: Dharma Publishing, 1977.

95. Ullman, Montague, M.D. *Working With Dreams.* New York: Random House Publishing, 1979.

96. Vaughan, Frances F. *Awakening Intuition.* Garden City, NY: Anchor Press/Doubleday, 1979.

97. Wanless, James. *Strategic Intuition for the 21st Century.* Carmel, CA: Merrill-West Publishing, 1997.

98. Warren, Rick. *The Purpose Driven Life.* Grand Rapids, MI: Zondervan, 2002.

99. Waters, Owen. *The Shift.* Delaware, MD: Infinite Being Publishing LLC, 2005.

100. Weil, Andrew. *Spontaneous Healing.* New York: Knopf, 1995.

101. Welfeld, Renee. *Your Body's Wisdom: A Body-Centered Approach to Transformation.* Naperville, IL: Sourcebooks, 1997.

102. Whitbourne, Susan K. and Willis, Sherry L. *The Baby Boomers Grow Up: Contemporary Perspectives on Midlife.* Mahwah, NJ: Lawrence Erlbaum Associates, Publishers, 2006.

103. White, Jim. *What's My Purpose? A Journey of Personal and Professional Growth.* Monterey, CA: JL White International, Inc, 2007.

104. Whyte, David. *The Heart Aroused: Poetry and the Preservation of the Soul in Corporate America.* New York: Currency/Doubleday, 1994.

105. Wright, Machaelle Small. *Dancing in the Shadows of the Moon.* Jeffersonton, VA: Perelandra, 1995.

106. Zimmerman, Jack and Coyle, Virginia. *The Way of Council,* 2nd Ed. USA: Bramble Books, 1996, 2009.

About Suzanne ~ Her Life Purpose Journey

Suzanne Strisower has 35+ years in the helping professions and has spent her whole life expressing her life purpose of "guiding and empowering people to improve the quality of their lives" in many diverse ways. Her career path has covered 17 different professional expressions—each one connected to her life purpose in some way. Her extensive background gives her the ability to serve a wide variety of clients. Now her goal is to streamline this process for clients by awakening their life purpose and fulfilling it in ways that use their true potential in personally meaningful ways.

Academically, Suzanne studied at John F. Kennedy University, first focusing her education in consciousness studies and human potential. Using her creative side years later, she earned a B.A. in Fine Arts–Interior Design and had a successful interior design career specializing in medical facilities. She started a trend of creating "environments that heal."

In 1988, professionally burned out, Suzanne began her life purpose journey to reassess her life and what was truly most important to her. She returned to her passion—helping people! Wanting more knowledge, she attained a Master's Degree in Counseling Psychology. She worked helping adolescents in residential treatment and became a clinical hypnotherapist in order to guide people through trauma, loss, and the resolution of unanswered questions as well as to connect with the spiritual dimensions through regression sessions.

A decade or so later, her guidance and creativity led to the channeling of a unique New Age rune oracle, *The Runes of the Four Realms* (available at http://www.InsightfulRunes.com), followed a decade later by her first completed spiritual feature film screenplay, *Shileah*. Her guide, Great Spirit, presented the opportunity to create and host a weekly conscious living radio show called "Living Well Talk Radio."

In 2006, wanting to work with professionals, Suzanne became a Professional Certified Life Coach to utilize all of her gifts, talents, expertise, and passion in one profession where she truly can be a catalyst for change in her clients' lives. Currently, she is in the process of completing several coaching projects to guide people in creating their "High Havingness™"—their "internal fulfillment AND external satisfaction."

Finally, she has synthesized and perfected what she has learned to create a holistic workbook, *111 Inspirational Life Purpose Quotes & Exercises to Find Your Purpose in Life*, which offers a step-by-step process that has successfully guided thousands of people to have spiritual awareness, discover their own life purpose, follow their inner guidance, and create an inner confidence and peacefulness in their lives. To purchase her workbook or learn more about her coaching services, visit her websites: http://wwwYourNextStepCoach.com and www.AwakentoYourLifePurpose.com.

As Eckhart Tolle would say about our "inner and outer purpose," Suzanne is expressing hers using her 4D and 5D intuition, clarity, creativity, and out-of-the-box thinking to help people discover and awaken their life purpose so they can "Live their Best Life by Expressing their Best Self!"

About Suzanne ~ Media Page

Media, Presentations and Publications

Suzanne is a radio show host who has appeared in the media including several radio and television interviews nationally. She has been a guest lecturer at major universities and has conducted CEU classes and workshops nationally. She is a published author and has been a contributing author to several other publications.

Presentations, Speaking Engagements & Publications

Living Well Talk Radio™, hosts several weekly conscious living radio shows
111 Inspirational Life Purpose Quotes and Exercises to Find Your Purpose in Life,
  a unique life purpose workbook
SHILEAH, complete spiritual feature film script, reality-based trilogy
Coaching an Inspired Profession, Lotus Guide, May/June 2007
Be Happy, Healthy and Wealthy, coauthored with Wake-Up Women
A Spirit Guided Life, contributing author to book Word Colors
What Are Runes? interview, KHSL TV Channel 12, Chico, CA
The Power of the Runes, 30-minute TV segment for "Adventures in Health"
On Hypnosis, Radio interviews in Ohio and California
Hypnosis and the Biblical World, Guest lecturer, University of Miami, Miami, FL
Understanding and the Release of Stress, CEU course for Nurses, Concord, CA
Your Inner World Connection with Nature, California Department of Forestry Event

Classes & Workshops

Find Your Inner and Outer Purpose in Life™, Butte College workshop, Chico, CA
Creating a Great Life Class™, 8-week course, Oroville Center for Spiritual Living, Oroville, CA
You Are R.I.P.E. for Change™, 4-week teleseminar series
Spiritual Awareness and Practice in Everyday Life™, weekly classes working with Spirit using tarot, dreams, chakras, runes, numerology, and other topics
Becoming a Full Human Being™ and Discovering Alchemy—The Inner Journey™ hypnotherapy workshops to find your life purpose and connect with your Higher Self

Credentials and Affiliations:

Professional Certified Coach (PCC), International Coach Federation
Life Purpose and Career Coach (CC), Life Purpose Institute
Certified Life Coach (CLC), Coach for Life
M.A., Counseling Psychology, Pacifica Graduate Institute
B.A., Interior Design, John F. Kennedy University
Certified Inspired Learning Facilitator
Certified Clinical Hypnotherapist
Certified Conflict Resolution Panelist

Awards and Recognitions

Who's Who of American Women, 1993

Suzanne's Products & Services

Available from www.YourNextStepCoach.com or www.AwakentoYourLifePurpose.com

Private Coaching & Group Coaching
- Private coaching for individuals wanting personal attention
- Group coaching on life purpose and quality-of-life topics

Psychic Readings and Consultations
- Private coaching
- Psychic and life purpose readings
- Chakra readings

Teleseminars & In-Person Classes and Workshops
- 4-week teleseminar series
  You Are R.I.P.E. for Change™
  Making Change Be Your Friend™
  Discover & Awaken Your Purpose in Life™
- 8-week "Creating a Great Life™" teleseminar series
- Creating a Great Life online course
- Discover Your Inner and Outer Purpose in Life™ workshops

Guided Visualizations & Meditations
- Meeting Your Future Self
- Moving through the Dimensions—Self to the Cosmos
- Experiencing Your Chakras & Beyond
- Finding Your Life Purpose
- Rainbow Light Journey

Books
- Be Happy, Healthy and Wealthy
- The Runes of the Four Realms
- 111 Inspirational Life Purpose Quotes and Exercises to Fid Your Purpose in Life
- One Hundred Eleven "Tweetable" Life Purpose Quotes: a Book of Original Thoughts

Suzanne is available for custom groups, workshops and retreats.

For more information:
Suzanne Strisower, M.A., PCC
http://www.YourNextStepCoach.com
http://www.AwakentoYourLifePurpose.com
Suzanne@YourNextStepCoach.com

www.ingramcontent.com/pod-product-compliance
Lightning Source LLC
Chambersburg PA
CBHW080502110426
42742CB00017B/2976